Some Common Pascal Programs

Some Common Pascal Programs

**Based on the book
Some Common BASIC Programs**

Published by
Osborne/McGraw-Hill
630 Bancroft Way
Berkeley, California 94710
U. S. A.

For information on translations and book distributors outside of the
U.S.A., please write Osborne/McGraw-Hill at the above address.

SOME COMMON PASCAL PROGRAMS

234567890 DLDL 8765432

ISBN 0-931988-73-X

Cover design by Peter Kunz

Contents

Introduction

These 76 programs solve common problems in the areas of finance, business, mathematics, statistics, and home budgeting. All programs are ready to be typed into your computer and run.

You don't have to be a programmer to use this book, but you must understand the subject matter of the programs. It is beyond the scope of this book to explain in detail where, when, how, or why you would use any of them. Of course, this does not mean that you must be a financial analyst to the use the Discount Commercial Paper program or a mathematician to use the Poisson Distribution program. There are sample runs and practice problems for each program. If you understand the applications well enough to know that the program may fit your needs, but you would like more information, you will find suggestions for further reading with most programs.

This book's secondary purpose is to show by example the wide range of subjects that lend themselves to computerization. All too often, computer users who have cut their teeth on entertainment computing have trouble coming up with ideas for practical computing. So, even if you don't see a program in this book that is exactly what you need, you may find it easier to invent your own practical applications after studying some of these.

As you look through the programs in this book, you may discover that you can use parts of the programs or some of the programming techniques in your own work. For example, this book includes functions for manipulating dates and character strings which can be amalgamated into other programs. You may even use an entire program as a component part of you own larger, more complex program. Some of these programs share code with programs in the book *Some Practical Pascal Programs,* also published by Osborne/McGraw-Hill.

Organization

Each program is accompanied by a discussion of the subject matter, the program information, the content and form of the output, and Program Notes. This material is followed by examples of how the program might be used in more or less real-life situations. The point of these examples is to help you imagine potential uses for the program. The examples demonstrate as many of the program features as they can in a moderate-sized problem. The sample run is next, showing the dialogue between the computer and the user when the program is used to solve the problem posed in the example. Compare the user's inputs and the computer's outputs in the sample run with the problem stated in the example. You should understand how you would use the program to solve a similar problem.

The text of the Pascal program comes next. To save typing, and to accommodate differences in the way that different implementations of Pascal receive interactive input, some procedures, functions, and type declarations (called Include files) used by several of the programs are printed only once in Appendices A and B. If you type them into a file you have created for this purpose, you can simply copy them into each program where they are needed, using your system text editor. Alternatively, most Pascal implementations allow you to tell the compiler where to find files that will be "Included" at specific places in your programs. See Appendix A for more information on Include files.

Lastly, we list references for most programs. Investigate these books and articles if you wish to read more about the subject matter of the program.

Pascal Compatibility

These programs have been written in a very conservative Pascal, acceptable to any implementation. To remove the worst potential problem—interactive input—all input to these programs is done through routines to be copied from Appendix B. This appendix contains suitable routines for the most common solutions to the problem of interactive input in Pascal. One set of routines is suitable for use with UCSD Pascal, including Apple Pascal. Another set of routines will work for any implementation using the Lazy-IO convention, in which characters are not read until the first time the program attempts to inspect them. By merely selecting the appropriate routine to type in, all the programs should run without modification on your system. See Appendix A for more information on the different implementations of Pascal.

None of these programs requires a mass storage device (disk or tape) for storing data. Thus, the widely varying methods for accessing data files in Pascal are not a problem. Of course, you will want to store the programs themselves on a tape or disk once you have typed them in. This is a fairly straightforward procedure that should be described in the manual for your computer system.

How to Use These Programs

Follow these procedures when you want to use one of the programs in this book:

1. Read the program write-up and familiarize yourself with how the program works. Consult the suggested reference material if you need a better understanding of the subject matter that the program addresses. Be sure that the program does what you need it to do before going any further.

2. Type the program listing into your computer. Make a note of any Include files you need to have available, and if you are directing your compiler to find them in separate files, be sure you use the syntax specified by your compiler. (See Appendix A for more information on this.) Look for any lines containing comments that you should know about. If a comment line says to omit the line unless you have a particular Pascal implementation (such as Apple Pascal) and you are not using that implementation, do not type in the line.

3. Check your program listing carefully for correctness. Not all typing errors are caught by the compiler.

4. Save the program on tape or disk. Do it *now,* before you run the program. If you do, you can retrieve your work if anything happens while the program is running. Remember, unless your editor keeps an audit trail or has some other unusual protective feature, you are always in danger of losing all the work until you save the program. With longer programs you may wish to save it after typing it in.

5. Determine whether the current program requires any Include files that have not been typed in for another program. Type in these new Include files and save them in separate files. If you have directed your compiler to Include from those files, be sure you give it the correct file names. If your text editor copies the Include files into your main program file, you may still want to keep separate copies of the Include files for each use in later programs.

6. Compile the program. If the compiler indicates any errors, double-check your typing and check that you used the correct Include files.

7. Run the example exactly as shown in the sample run. If you have done everything right up to this point, the results should be similar to those published in the example. Your answers will differ slightly from those in the book if your computer has a different level of internal numerical precision than ours.
   NOTE: Most versions of UCSD Pascal have only six digits of precision for real numbers. This may lead to slight inaccuracies (in the cents columns) in financial calculations. If absolute accuracy is required, you might consider learning how to use the non-standard Long Integer feature and keeping monetary amounts in cents or mills.

8. If your answers differ markedly from ours, or your program does not run at all (that is, you get some sort of error message), it is time for some detective work. First, double-check your listing. It may be useful to count the number of lines, just to make sure that you have not duplicated or eliminated any lines, a common error. If you are still having trouble, read Appendix A for information on potential problems with implementation of Pascal.

9. By now your program should be running correctly. If not, have someone else look at your program. Often another pair of eyes can see something that you repeatedly miss. Try putting the program aside for a while and come back to it after a short break. Errors you didn't see before may be obvious later.

Acknowledgments

These programs are Pascal versions of BASIC programs originally published in *Some Common BASIC Programs* (Osborne/McGraw-Hill, 1977). Gregory Davidson converted 41 of the original BASIC programs. The remaining 35 were written by Osborne/McGraw-Hill staff programmers Brad Hellman, Brian Williamson, and Vicki Marney-Petix, and the book was edited by Vicki Marney-Petix. The original *Some Common BASIC Programs* was edited by Lon Poole and Mary Borchers.

1

Future Value of an Investment

This program calculates the future value of an investment which earns interest. You must know the amount of the initial investment, the nominal interest rate, the number of compounding periods per year, and the amount of time in months and years that the money is invested.

A financial situation may act like a compound interest calculation even when it is called something else. A steady rise in property values is a good example. Please note that if there is only one compounding period per year, you must specify a term in whole years to obtain an accurate answer.

Assuming there are no additional deposits and no withdrawals, the future value is based on the formula

$$T = P\,(1 + i/N)^{N \cdot Y}$$

where: T = total value after Y years (future value)
P = initial investment
i = nominal interest rate
N = number of compounding periods per year
Y = number of years

Examples:

Carl makes an investment of $6800.00 at 9.5%. If interest is compounded quarterly, what will be the value of Carl's investment in 10 years and 6 months?

Valerie purchases a piece of property for $16,050.00. Property values are rising at an average annual rate of 7%. What may Valerie expect her property to be worth in five years?

Run:

```
Future value of an investment

Initial investment: $6800
Nominal interest rate (%) 9.5
Number of compounding periods per year: 4
Number of whole years: 10
Number of periods past last whole year: 0
Future value = $ 17388.6

Would you like another run? (y/n) y

Initial investment: $16050
Nominal interest rate (%) 7
Number of compounding periods per year: 1
Number of whole years: 5.5
Number of periods past last whole year: 0
Future value = $ 22511.0

Would you like another run? (y/n) n
```

Program Listing:

```pascal
program FutureVal(input, output);
var
  NumPeriods, XtraPeriods, NumYears: integer;
  investment, percent, rate: real;

{$I IntRaise}
{$I NotAgain}

begin { main }
  writeln('Future value of an investment');
  repeat
    writeln;
    write('Initial investment: $');
    readln(investment);
    write('Nominal interest rate (%) ');
    readln(percent);
    write('Number of compounding periods per year: ');
    readln(NumPeriods);
    write('Number of whole years: ');
    readln(NumYears);
    write('Number of periods past last whole year: ');
    readln(XtraPeriods);
    rate := percent / NumPeriods / 100;
    writeln('Future value = $', investment
        * IntRaise(1 + rate, NumPeriods * NumYears + XtraPeriods):9:2);
    writeln
  until NotAgain
end.
```

2
Future Value of Regular Deposits (Annuity)

This program calculates a future value when regular deposits are made. You must provide the amount of each deposit, the number of deposits per year, the amount of time the future value is calculated for, and the nominal interest rate.

Assuming that interest is compounded with each deposit, the calculation is based on the formula

$$T = R \cdot \left(\frac{(1 + i/n)^{N \cdot Y} - 1}{i/N} \right)$$

where: T = total value after Y years (future value)
R = amount of regular deposits
N = number of deposits per year
Y = number of years
i = nominal interest rate

Examples:

Michel makes annuity payments of $175.00. The interest is 5.5%. What amount will Michel have accumulated in 15 years?

Each month, Tanya transfers $50 from her checking account to a Christmas Club savings account with 5% interest. How much can Tanya expect to have saved at the end of the year?

Run:

```
Future Value of Regular Deposits (Annuity)

Amount of regular deposits: $50
Nominal interest rate: (%) 5
Number of deposits per year: 12
Number of years: 1
Future value = $    613.95

Would you like another run? (y/n) y

Amount of regular deposits: $175
Nominal interest rate: (%) 5.5
Number of deposits per year: 1
Number of years: 15
Future value = $  3921.51

Would you like another run? (y/n) n
```

Program Listing:

```
program annuity(input, output);
var
   DepsPerYear, NumYears: integer;
   AmtDep, percent, RatePerDep: real;

{$I IntRaise}
{$I NotAgain}

begin { main }
   writeln('Future Value of Regular Deposits (Annuity)');
   repeat
     writeln;
     write('Amount of regular deposits: $');
     readln(AmtDep);
     write('Nominal interest rate: (%) ');
     readln(percent);
     write('Number of deposits per year: ');
     readln(DepsPerYear);
     write('Number of years: ');
     readln(NumYears);
     RatePerDep := percent / DepsPerYear / 100;
     writeln('Future value = $', AmtDep
             * (IntRaise(1 + RatePerDep, DepsPerYear * NumYears) - 1
             / RatePerDep:9:2);
     writeln
   until NotAgain
end.
```

3
Regular Deposits

This program calculates the regular deposit amount required to provide a stated future value in a specified time period. All deposits are equal, and the number of deposits per year must be at least one. You must know the future value, the nominal interest rate, the number of deposits per year, and the term in years and months.

You must be careful to input only terms that are "reasonable" for the specified problem. For example, if deposits are quarterly and you specify a term of two years and two months, the answer will be prorated on the basis of the next quarterly deposit. But, financial institutions do not prorate. A term of two years and two months would be reasonable if deposits were monthly, however.

The calculation for regular deposits is based on the formula

$$R = T \left(\frac{i/N}{(1 + i/N)^{N \cdot Y} - 1} \right)$$

where: R = amount of regular deposit
T = future value
i = nominal interest rate
N = number of deposits per year
Y = number of years

Examples:

Karen would like to have $1000 in her savings account at the end of the year. How much must she deposit each month to reach her goal, if she is receiving 8% interest on her savings?

Roman has opened an Individual Retirement Account (IRA) which he hopes will have $15,000 in 10 years and 3 months. The nominal interest rate for IRAs at his bank is 12.5% and he will make quarterly deposits. How large must each deposit be?

Run:

```
Regular Deposits

Desired future value: $1000
Nominal interest rate: (%) 8
Number of deposits per year? 12
Number of whole years: 1
Number of additional months(0-12): 0

Regular deposits = $  80.32

Would you like another run? (y/n) y

Desired future value: $15000
Nominal interest rate: (%) 12.5
Number of deposits per year? 4
Number of whole years: 10
Number of additional months(0-12): 3

Regular deposits = $ 185.19

Would you like another run? (y/n) n
```

Program Listing:

```pascal
program RegularDeposits(input, output);
uses transcendentals;{omit this line if not Apple Pascal}
var
   NumYears, NumMonths, DepsPerYear: integer;
   value, percent, RatePerDep, TotalTime: real;

{$I RealRaise}
{$I ReadInt}
{$I NotAgain}

begin { main }
   writeln('Regular Deposits');
   repeat
     writeln;
     write('Desired future value: $');
     readln(value);
     write('Nominal interest rate: (%) ');
     readln(percent);
     repeat
       write('Number of deposits per year? ')
     until ReadInt(DepsPerYear, 1, maxint);
     repeat
       write('Number of whole years: ')
     until ReadInt(NumYears, 1, maxint);
     repeat
       write('Number of additional months(0-12): ')
     until ReadInt(NumMonths,0,12);
     RatePerDep := percent / DepsPerYear / 100;
     TotalTime:=NumYears+NumMonths/12;
     writeln;
     writeln('Regular deposits = $',
             value * RatePerDep
             /(RealRaise(RatePerDep + 1, DepsPerYear * TotalTime) - 1):7:2);
     writeln
   until NotAgain
end.
```

4
Regular Withdrawals from an Investment

This program calculates the maximum amount that may be withdrawn regularly from an investment over a specified time period, leaving a zero balance in the account. All withdrawals are equal. If less than the maximum amount is withdrawn, a balance will remain in the account at the end of the time period. You must know the amount of the initial investment, the nominal interest rate, the number of withdrawals per year, and the term in years and months.

You must be careful to input only terms that are "reasonable" for the specified problem. For example, if withdrawals are quarterly and you specify a term of two years and two months, the answer will be prorated on the basis of the next quarterly withdrawal. But, financial institutions do not prorate. A term of two years and two months would be perfectly reasonable if withdrawals were monthly, however.

The maximum amount of the withdrawals is calculated using the formula

$$R = P \left(\frac{i/N}{(1 + i/N)^{N \cdot Y} - 1} + \frac{i}{N} \right)$$

where: R = amount of regular withdrawal
P = initial investment
i = nominal interest rate
N = number of withdrawals per year
Y = number of years

Examples:

The twins, David and Daniel, each received legacies of $8000 from their aunt's estate. They invested their money with a nominal interest rate of 9.5%. David wants to make regular monthly withdrawals for ten years. What is the maximum he can withdraw each month?

Daniel wants to make weekly withdrawals from his account for ten years and six months. What is the maximum amount he can withdraw each week?

Run:

```
Regular Withdrawals from an Investment

Initial investment: $8000
Nominal interest rate: (%) 9.5
Number of withdrawals per year: 12
Number of whole years: 10
Number of additional months(0-12): 0
Amount of each withdrawal = $ 103.52

Would you like another run? (y/n) n
```

Program Listing:

```
program RegularWithdrawals(input, output);
uses transcend;  { Omit this line if not using Apple Pascal }
var
  WithsPerYear, NumYears, NumMonths: integer;
  invest, percent, RatePerWith, TotalTime: real;
```

7

```
{$I ReadInt}
{$I RealRaise}
{$I NotAgain}

begin { main }
  writeln('Regular Withdrawals from an Investment');
  repeat
    writeln;
    write('Initial investment: $');
    readln(invest);
    write('Nominal interest rate: (%) ');
    readln(percent);
    repeat
      write('Number of withdrawals per year: ')
    until ReadInt(WithsPerYear, 1, maxint);
    repeat
      write('Number of whole years: ')
    until ReadInt(NumYears, 1, maxint);
    repeat
      write('Number of additional months(0-12): ')
    until ReadInt(NumMonths,0,12);
    RatePerWith := percent / WithsPerYear / 100;
    TotalTime:=NumYears + NumMonths/12;
    writeln('Amount of each withdrawal = $', invest *
            (RatePerWith / (RealRaise(RatePerWith + 1,
            WithsPerYear * TotalTime) - 1)
            + RatePerWith):6:2);
      writeln
  until NotAgain
  end.
```

5
Initial Investment

This program calculates the investment necessary to provide a stated future value in a specified time period. You must enter the future value of the investment, the term of the investment in months and years, the number of compounding periods per year, and the nominal interest rate.

You must be careful to input only terms that are "reasonable" for the specified problem. For example, if compounding is quarterly and you specify a term of two years and two months, the answer will be prorated on the basis of the next quarterly compounding. But financial institutions do not prorate. A term of two years and two months would be reasonable if compounding were monthly, however.

The formula used to calculate the initial investment is

$$P = \frac{T}{(1 + i/N)^{N \cdot Y}}$$

where: P = initial investment
T = future value
N = number of compounding periods per year
Y = number of years
i = nominal interest rate

Examples:

Ernie wants to have $10,000 saved at the end of ten years. His bank offers him 8.5% interest with interest compounded quarterly. What must his initial investment be?

Merchant Savings and Loan wishes to sell a bond which will be worth $5000 five years from the purchase date. Interest will be 7.9% compounded daily. How much must the bank charge for the bond? (**NOTE:** Daily compounding, because it involves 365 calculations per year, will be most affected by differences in the numerical precision of a particular machine.)

Run:

```
Initial Investment

Desired future value: $10000
Number of compounding periods per year: 4
Number of whole years: 10
Number of additional months(0-12): 0
Nominal interest rate: (%) 8.5

Initial investment = $ 4312.38

Would you like another run? (y/n) y

Desired future value: $5000
Number of compounding periods per year: 365
Number of whole years: 5
Number of additional months(0-12): 0
Nominal interest rate: (%) 7.9
```

```
Initial investment = $ 3368.26

Would you like another run? (y/n) n
```

Program Listing:

```pascal
program InitialInvestment(input, output);
uses transcend;    { Omit this line if not using Apple Pascal}
var
   NumPeriods, NumYears, NumMonths: integer;
   value, percent, RatePerPeriod,TotalTime: real;

{$I ReadInt}
{$I RealRaise}
{$I NotAgain}

begin { main }
   writeln('Initial Investment');
   repeat
     writeln;
     write('Desired future value: $');
     readln(value);
     repeat
       write('Number of compounding periods per year: ')
     until ReadInt(NumPeriods, 1, maxint);
     repeat
       write('Number of whole years: ')
     until ReadInt(NumYears, 1, maxint);
     repeat
       write('Number of additional months(0-12): ')
     until ReadInt(NumMonths,0,12);
     write('Nominal interest rate: (%) ');
     readln(percent);
     RatePerPeriod := percent / NumPeriods / 100;
     TotalTime:=NumYears + NumMonths/12;
     writeln;
     writeln('Initial investment = $', value /
             RealRaise(RatePerPeriod + 1, NumPeriods * TotalTime):6:2);
     writeln
   until NotAgain
end.
```

6
Minimum Investment for Withdrawals

This program calculates the minimum investment required to allow regular withdrawals over a specified time period. You must know the amount of each withdrawal, the number of withdrawals per year, the term in years and months, and the nominal interest rate on the investment. All withdrawals are equal. If you withdraw less than the calculated maximum amount on any occasion, you will have a remainder in your account at the close of the term. Additionally, if you invest more than the amount calculated as the minimum initial investment, you will complete the term with a remainder in your account.

   You must be careful to input only terms that are "reasonable" for the specified problem. For example, if withdrawals are quarterly and you specify a term of two years and two months, the answer will be prorated on the basis of the next quarterly withdrawal. But, financial institutions do not prorate. A term of two years and two months would be reasonable if withdrawals were monthly, however.

   Assuming that interest is compounded with each withdrawal, the calculation is based on the formula

$$P = \frac{R \cdot N}{i} \left(1 - \frac{1}{(1 + i/N)^{N \cdot Y}} \right)$$

where: P = initial investment
R = amount of regular withdrawal
i = nominal interest rate
N = number of withdrawals per year
Y = number of years

Examples:

Tony and Maybeth wish to invest a sum at 6% interest and withdraw $100 per month for five years. What is the minimum investment they must make?

   Solange wishes to withdraw $250 per month for six years and five months. The credit union will pay her 6% interest on her investment. What is the minimum amount she must invest?

Run:

```
Minimum Investment for Withdrawals

Amount of withdrawals: $100
Nominal interest rate: (%) 6
Number of withdrawals per year: 12
Number of whole years: 5
Number of additional months(0-12): 0

Minimum investment = $ 5172.55

Would you like another run? (y/n) n
```

Program Listing:

```pascal
program MinInvestWithdrawals(input, output);
uses transcend;   { Omit this line if not using Apple Pascal }
var
  WithsPerYear, NumYears, NumMonths: integer;
  amount, percent, rate, TotalTime: real;

{$I ReadInt}
{$I RealRaise}
{$I NotAgain}

begin { main }
  writeln('Minimum Investment for Withdrawals');
  repeat
    writeln;
    write('Amount of withdrawals: $');
    readln(amount);
    write('Nominal interest rate: (%) ');
    readln(percent);
    repeat
      write('Number of withdrawals per year: ')
    until ReadInt(WithsPerYear, 1, maxint);
    repeat
      write('Number of whole years: ')
    until ReadInt(NumYears, 1, maxint);
    repeat
      write('Number of additional months(0-12): ')
    until ReadInt(NumMonths, 0, 12);
    writeln;
    TotalTime:=NumYears + NumMonths/12;
    rate := percent / WithsPerYear / 100;
    writeln('Minimum investment = $',
            amount / rate
            * (1 - 1/RealRaise(rate + 1, WithsPerYear * TotalTime)):6:2);
    writeln
  until NotAgain
end.
```

7
Nominal Interest Rate on Investments

This program calculates the nominal interest rate when you provide the initial investment, the term in months and years, and the future value of the investment. The nominal rate is a constant for the term of the investment.

The nominal interest rate is usually subdivided for compounding purposes.

"Nominal Interest Rate" is based on the formula

$$i = N (T/P)^{\frac{1}{N \cdot Y}} - N$$

where: i = nominal interest rate
P = initial investment
T = future value
N = number of compounding periods per year
Y = number of years

The nominal interest rate is expressed as a yearly rate even though the interest rate used when compounding interest is i/N. The nominal interest rate will be less than the effective interest rate when interest is compounded more than once a year. This is because the nominal rate does not take into account interest compounded on interest earned in earlier periods of each year. For example, the schedule of earned interest on $100 at 5% compounded quarterly would be

Period	Balance	$\dfrac{i/100}{N}$		Interest	New Balance
1	$100.00 •	0.0125	=	$1.25	$101.25
2	$101.25 •	0.0125	=	$1.27	$102.52
3	$102.52 •	0.0125	=	$1.28	$103.80
4	$103.80 •	0.0125	=	$1.30	$105.10

The *effective* interest rate in the example is 5.1%, although the *nominal* rate is 5%.

You must be careful to input only terms that are "reasonable" for the specified problem. For example, if compounding is quarterly and you specify a term of two years and two months, the answer will be prorated on the basis of the next quarterly compounding. But financial institutions do not prorate. A term of two years and two months would be reasonable if compounding were monthly, however.

Examples:

Richard invests $945.00 in his credit union. Four and a half years later, his investment amounts to $1309.79. If interest is compounded monthly, what was the nominal interest rate at the credit union during that time?

Cesar invests $3000.00 and ten years later he has earned $1576.00 interest. If interest is compounded monthly, what is the nominal interest rate on the account?

Run:

```
Nominal Interest Rate on Investments

Principal: $945
```

```
Future value: $1309.79
Number of whole years: 4
Number of additional months(0-12): 6
Number of compounding periods per year: 12

Nominal interest rate = 7.28%

Would you like another run? (y/n) y

Principal: $3000
Future value: $4576
Number of whole years: 4
Number of additional months(0-12): 0
Number of compounding periods per year: 12

Nominal interest rate =  10.60%

Would you like another run? (y/n) n
```

Program Listing:

```pascal
program NominalInterestRate(input, output);
uses transcendentals; { omit this line if not using Apple Pascal }
var
  NumPeriods, NumYears, NumMonths:integer;
  principal, value, TotalTime:real;

{$I ReadInt}
{$I RealRaise}
{$I NotAgain}

begin { main }
  writeln('Nominal Interest Rate on Investments');
  repeat
    writeln;
    write('Principal: $');
    readln(principal);
    write('Future value: $');
    readln(value);
    repeat
      write('Number of whole years: ')
    until ReadInt(NumYears,0,maxint);
    repeat
      write('Number of additional months(0-12): ')
    until ReadInt(NumMonths,0,12);
    repeat
      write('Number of compounding periods per year: ')
    until ReadInt(NumPeriods, 1, maxint);
    writeln;
    TotalTime:=NumYears + NumMonths/12;
    writeln('Nominal interest rate = ', NumPeriods
            * (RealRaise(value / principal,
            1/(NumPeriods * TotalTime)) - 1)
            * 100:5:2, '%');
    writeln
  until NotAgain
end.
```

8
Effective Interest Rate on Investments

This program calculates the effective interest rate on an investment, which is the actual interest rate the investment earns. You must provide the amounts of the initial and final investments and the term in years and months.

The effective interest rate is calculated with the formula

$$\text{effective interest rate} = \left(\frac{\text{future value}}{\text{initial investment}} \right)^{1/\text{years}} - 1$$

You can use this program to calculate the effective rate on investments you have already made, or to calculate the rate of interest you must earn in order to turn a proposed initial investment into a desired future value in the specified time. After you have calculated the effective interest rate you must earn to achieve your goals, you can shop around for an appropriate investment. You can also use this program to calculate an effective depreciation rate. The depreciation rate is expressed as a negative annual interest rate.

Examples:

Kathleen has decided to deposit $945.00 in her credit union. Four years and six months later her account has a balance of $1309.79. What actual percent of her initial investment did the credit union pay her annually during that time?

Seamus bought his car for $7534.84 in 1978 and sold it in 1981 for $3555.00. What was the effective rate of depreciation?

Run:

```
Effective Interest Rate on Investments

Initial investment: $945
Future value: $1309.79
Number of whole years: 4
Additional number of months(0-12): 6

Annual interest rate =  7.52%

Would you like another run? (y/n) y

Initial investment: $7534.84
Future value: $3555
Number of whole years: 3
Additional number of months(0-12): 0

Annual interest rate = -22.15%

Would you like another run? (y/n) n
```

Program Listing:

```
program EffectIntRate(input, output);
uses transcendentals; { omit this line if not using Apple Pascal }
var
   NumYears, NumMonths: integer;
   investment, value, TotalTime: real;

{$I RealRaise}
{$I NotAgain}
{$I ReadInt}

begin { main }
   writeln('Effective Interest Rate on Investments');
   repeat
     writeln;
     write('Initial investment: $');
     readln(investment);
     write('Future value: $');
     readln(value);
     repeat
       write('Number of whole years: ')
     until ReadInt(NumYears,0,maxint);
     repeat
       write('Additional number of months(0-12): ')
     until ReadInt(NumMonths,0,12);
     writeln;
     TotalTime:= NumYears + NumMonths/12;
     writeln('Annual interest rate = ',
             (RealRaise(value / investment, 1/TotalTime) - 1)
             * 100:5:2, '%');
     writeln
   until NotAgain
end.
```

9
Earned Interest Table

This program calculates and prints an earned interest table for investments. The schedule contains

1. Periodic balance
2. Interest accumulated in the latest compounding period
3. Total interest accumulated
4. Effective interest rate.

These may be calculated for a single investment or for an initial investment with regular deposits or withdrawals. If the table will tabulate a single investment, you must provide the amount of the initial investment, the nominal interest rate, and the number of compounding periods per year. Your new balance will be printed a maximum of four times per year. If interest is compounded less than four times per year, your new balance will be posted with each interest calculation.

If the table is tabulated for regular deposits or withdrawals, you must provide the amount of the initial investment, the nominal interest rate, and the number and amount of deposits or withdrawals per year. In this case, interest is compounded daily with a 360-day year. Your new balance will be printed at each deposit or withdrawal.

Examples:

Toni invests $2000 at 9.5% interest in a trust fund for her niece for ten years. Interest is compounded monthly. What is her yearly balance and earned interest for the final two years of the investment?

Joshua deposits $1000 at 8% in his credit union. Every month he deposits $50 from payroll deduction. What is the earned interest table for the first year of this savings plan?

Teresa deposits $1000 at 8% in her credit union. Every quarter she withdraws $150. What is the earned interest table for the first year of this plan?

Run:

```
Earned Interest Table

Principal: $2000
Nominal Interest Rate: (%) 9.5
Number of deposits/withdrawals per year: 0
Number of compounding periods per year: 12
Start with what year: 9
End printing with what year: 10

        Calculating table...

              Earned Interest Table
   Principal $ 2000.00     at 9.50% Nominal        for 10 years
        Effective Interest Rate 9.92 % per year

Year    Balance         Interest        Accum. Interest

9
        4365.87         2365.87         2365.87
        4470.38          104.51         2470.38
        4577.39          107.01         2577.39
        4686.97          109.58         2686.97
```

10

4799.17	112.20	2799.17
4914.06	114.89	2914.06
5031.70	117.64	3031.70
5152.15	120.45	3152.15

Would you like another run? (y/n) y

Principal: $1000
Nominal Interest Rate: (%) 8
Number of deposits/withdrawals per year: 12
Amount of deposit/withdrawal: $50
Start with what year: 1
End printing with what year: 1

                    Earned Interest Table
    Principal $ 1000.00   at 8.00% Nominal   for 1 years
Regular Deposit/Withdrawal $ 50.00   12 Times per year
        Effective Interest Rate 8.33 % per year

Year	Balance	Interest	Accum. Interest
1			
	1056.70	6.70	6.70
	1113.78	7.08	13.78
	1171.24	7.46	21.24
	1229.08	7.84	29.08
	1287.31	8.23	37.31
	1345.93	8.62	45.93
	1404.94	9.01	54.94
	1464.35	9.41	64.35
	1524.15	9.80	74.15
	1584.35	10.20	84.35
	1644.96	10.61	94.96
	1705.97	11.01	105.97

Would you like another run? (y/n) y

Principal: $1000
Nominal Interest Rate: (%) 8
Number of deposits/withdrawals per year: 4
Amount of deposit/withdrawal: $-150
Start with what year: 1
End printing with what year: 1

                    Earned Interest Table
    Principal $ 1000.00   at 8.00% Nominal   for 1 years
Regular Deposit/Withdrawal $-150.00   4 Times per year
        Effective Interest Rate 8.33 % per year

Year	Balance	Interest	Accum. Interest
1			
	870.16	20.16	20.16
	737.70	17.54	37.70
	602.57	14.87	52.57
	464.71	12.14	64.71

Would you like another run? (y/n) n

Program Listing:

```
program Earnedint(input,output);
const
   MaxDigits = 6;
   LinesPerPage = 66;
   FinishLine = 55;
   StartLine = 6;
var
   StartYear, EndYear : integer;
   NumTrans, NumPeriods, PrintsPerYear : integer;
   Rate, Principle, AmtTrans : real;

   {$I ReadReal}
   {$I GetPercent}
   {$I ReadInt}
   {$I IntRaise}
   {$I RealTrunc}
   {$I RealRound}
   {$I NotAgain}

   procedure PrintTable;
   const
      NumPosts = 4;
   var
      CurLine, NumPrints, CurPeriod, CurYear, CurPosting, CurTrans: integer;
      Balance, BalPlusInt, IntEachPeriod, AccumInt, Interest: real;
   begin
      Balance := Principle;
      IntEachPeriod := 0;
      AccumInt := 0;
      Interest := 0;
      CurLine := LinesPerPage;
      CurYear := 0;
      if StartYear > 1 then
        begin
          writeln; writeln('        Calculating table...')
        end;
      repeat { For CurYear := 1 to EndYear + 1 or no more lines in last year }
        CurYear := CurYear + 1;
        if CurYear >= StartYear then
          begin
            if CurLine >= FinishLine then
              begin
                for CurLine := CurLine to LinesPerPage do
                  writeln;
                CurLine := StartLine;
                writeln('Earned Interest Table':40);
                writeln('  Principal $',Principle:MaxDigits:2,'     at',
                        Rate*100:5:2,'% Nominal        for ',EndYear:0,' years');
                if NumTrans <> 0 then
                  begin
                    writeln('Regular Deposit/Withdrawal $',
                            AmtTrans:MaxDigits:2, '      ',
                            NumTrans:0, ' Times per year');
                    CurLine := CurLine + 1
                  end; { If NumTrans <> 0 }
                writeln('Effective Interest Rate':30, 100 *
                        (Intraise(1 + Rate / NumPeriods, NumPeriods) - 1):5:2,
                        ' % per year');
                writeln;
                writeln('Year', 'Balance':11,
```

```
                        'Interest':15, 'Accum. Interest':22);
              writeln
            end; { If CurLine >= FinishLine }
          writeln (CurYear);
        end; { if CurYear >= StartYear }
      NumPrints := 1;
      CurTrans := 1;
      CurPosting := 1;
      CurPeriod := 1;
      repeat { CurPeriod := 1 to NumPeriods or no more lines in last year
        if CurTrans <= NumTrans then
          if CurTrans / NumTrans <= CurPeriod / NumPeriods then
            begin
              Balance := Balance + AmtTrans;
              CurTrans := CurTrans + 1
            end;
        BalPlusInt := Balance * (1 + Rate / NumPeriods);
        IntEachPeriod := BalPlusInt - Balance;
        Interest := Interest + IntEachPeriod;
        AccumInt := AccumInt + IntEachPeriod;
        if CurPosting / NumPosts <= CurPeriod / NumPeriods then
          begin
            AccumInt := RealRound(AccumInt, 2);
            BalPlusInt := RealRound (BalPlusInt,2);
            CurPosting := CurPosting + 1
          end;
        if CurYear >= StartYear then
          if CurPeriod / Numperiods >= NumPrints / PrintsPerYear then
            begin
              NumPrints := NumPrints + 1;
              writeln(BalPlusInt:15:2,Interest:15:2,AccumInt:15:2);
              Interest := 0;
              CurLine := CurLine + 1
            end;  { CurPeriod / Numperiods >= NumPrints / PrintsPerYear}
        Balance := BalPlusInt;
        CurPeriod := CurPeriod + 1
      until (CurPeriod > NumPeriods) or
            (CurYear + CurPeriod / NumPeriods - 1 > EndYear);
    if CurYear >= StartYear then
      begin
        writeln;
        CurLine := CurLine + 1
      end;
  until (CurYear > (EndYear + 1)) or
  (CurYear + CurPeriod / NumPeriods - 1 >= EndYear)
end; { Print Table }

  begin  { main }
    writeln('Earned Interest Table');
    repeat
      writeln;
      repeat
        write('Principal: $')
      until ReadReal(Principle);
      repeat
        write('Nominal Interest Rate')
      until GetPercent(Rate);
      repeat
        write('Number of deposits/withdrawals per year: ');
      until ReadInt(NumTrans,0,MaxInt);
```

```
        if NumTrans <> 0 then
          begin
          repeat
            write('Amount of deposit/withdrawal: $');
          until ReadReal (AmtTrans);
          NumPeriods := 360;
          PrintsPerYear := NumTrans
        end
      else
        begin
        repeat
          write('Number of compounding periods per year: ');
        until ReadInt(NumPeriods,1,360);
        NumTrans := 0;
        PrintsPerYear := 4
        end;

        repeat
          write('Start with what year: ')
        until ReadInt(StartYear,1,MaxInt);
        repeat
          write('End printing with what year: ');
        until ReadInt(EndYear,1,MaxInt);
        PrintTable;
        writeln
  until NotAgain
end.
```

10
Depreciation Rate

This program calculates the annual depreciation rate of an investment. You must provide the original price of the item, its resale price, and its age in years.

The depreciation rate is calculated by the formula

$$\frac{\text{depreciation}}{\text{rate}} = 1 - \left(\frac{\text{resale price}}{\text{original price}}\right)^{1/\text{age}}$$

Example:

Jon bought his car for $4933.76 and sold it for $2400.00 three years later. What was its annual depreciation rate?

Run:

```
Depreciation Rate

Original price: $4933.76
Resale Price: $2400
Age: (whole years) 3
Age: (additional months(0-12)) 0

Depreciation rate =  21.35%

Would you like another run? (y/n) n
```

Program Listing:

```
program DepreciationRate(input, output);
uses transcendentals; { omit this line if not using Apple Pascal }
const digits = 2;
var  NumYears,NumMonths: integer;
     original, resale, age: real;

{$I RealRaise}
{$I NotAgain}
{$I ReadInt}

begin { main }
  writeln('Depreciation Rate');
  repeat
    writeln;
    write('Original price: $');
    readln(original);
    write('Resale Price: $');
    readln(resale);
    repeat
      write('Age: (whole years) ')
    until ReadInt(NumYears,0,maxint);
    repeat
```

22

```
        write('Age: (additional months(0-12)) ')
    until ReadInt(NumMonths,0,12);
    age:= NumYears + NumMonths/12;
    writeln;
    writeln('Depreciation rate = ',
        (1 - RealRaise(resale / original, 1/age)) * 100:3+digits:digits, '%');
    writeln
  until NotAgain
end.
```

11
Depreciation Amount

This program calculates the dollar amount of the depreciation, year by year, for an investment whose value decreases over time. You must know the annual rate of depreciation, the original cost of the investment, and the year of the depreciation.

The depreciation amount is calculated by the formula

$$D = P \cdot i \cdot (1 - i)^{Y - 1}$$

where: D = depreciation amount
P = original price
i = depreciation rate
Y = year of depreciation

Examples:

Marc bought his car for $4933.76. It depreciates at an annual rate of 21%. What is the dollar amount of the depreciation for the first three years?

His sister Sarah has a tape deck in her car. It cost $155 two years ago and has an annual depreciation rate of 22%. What is the dollar amount of the depreciation in the third year?

Run:

```
Depreciation Amount

Original price: $4933.76
Depreciation rate: (%) 21
Enter in age values, enter 0 when done:
Age: (whole years) 1
Depreciation =  1036.09

Age: (whole years) 2
Depreciation =  818.51

Age: (whole years) 3
Depreciation =  646.62

Age: (whole years) 0

Would you like another run? (y/n) y

Original price: $155
Depreciation rate: (%) 22
Enter in age values, enter 0 when done:
Age: (whole years) 3
Depreciation =  20.75

Age: (whole years) 0

Would you like another run? (y/n) n
```

Program Listing:

```
program DepreciationAmount(input, output);
const
  digits = 2;
var
  age: integer;
  original, rate: real;

{$I ReadInt}
{$I ReadReal}
{$I IntRaise}
{$I NotAgain}

begin { main }
  writeln('Depreciation Amount');
  repeat
    writeln;
    repeat
      write('Original price: $');
    until ReadReal(original);
    repeat
      write('Depreciation rate: (%) ')
    until ReadReal(rate);
    rate := rate / 100;
    writeln('Enter in age values, enter 0 when done:');
    repeat
      write('Age: (whole years) ')
    until ReadInt(age, 0, maxint);
    while age <> 0 do
      begin
        writeln('Depreciation = ',
          original * rate * IntRaise(1 - rate, age - 1):3+digits:digits);
        writeln;
        repeat
          write('Age: (whole years) ')
        until ReadInt(age, 0, maxint)
      end;
    writeln
  until NotAgain
end.
```

12
Salvage Value

This program calculates the salvage value of an item at the end of a given year of depreciation. You must know the salvage value of the item, its original price, and its depreciation rate.

The salvage value is obtained by the formula

$$S = P(1 - i)^Y$$

where: S = salvage value
P = original price
i = depreciation rate
Y = age in years

Examples:

What is the salvage value of Vonda's car if it is three years old, cost $4933.76, and depreciates at 21% annually? What would its salvage value be at the end of another year?

Vonda's tape deck is two years old. What is its present value if it cost $155.00 originally and depreciates at an annual rate of 22%?

Run:

```
Salvage Value

Original price: $4933.76
Depreciation rate: 21
Enter 0 when you have no more ages.
Age: (whole years) 3
Salvage value = $ 2432.54

Age: (whole years) 4
Salvage value = $ 1921.70

Age: (whole years) 0

Would you like another run? (y/n) y

Original price: $155
Depreciation rate: 22
Enter 0 when you have no more ages.
Age: (whole years) 2
Salvage value = $ 94.30

Age: (whole years) 0

Would you like another run? (y/n) n
```

Program Listing:

```pascal
program SalvageValue(input, output);
var
  age: integer;
  original, rate: real;

{$I ReadInt}
{$I IntRaise}
{$I NotAgain}

begin { main }
  writeln('Salvage Value');
  repeat
    writeln;
    write('Original price: $');
    readln(original);
    write('Depreciation rate: ');
    readln(rate);
    rate := rate / 100; { percent -> fraction }
    writeln('Enter 0 when you have no more ages.');
    repeat
      write('Age: (whole years) ')
    until ReadInt(age, 0, maxint);
    while age <> 0 do
      begin
        writeln('Salvage value = $', original
        * IntRaise(1 - rate, age):6:2);
        writeln;
        repeat
          write('Age: (whole years) ')
        until ReadInt(age, 0, maxint)
      end;
    writeln
  until NotAgain
end.
```

13
Discount Commercial Paper

This program calculates the amount of discount and the net cost of a discounted commerical paper. You must know the future value of the paper, the discount rate, and the number of days to maturity.

The formulas used to calculate the discount and cost are as follows:

$$\text{discount} = T \cdot \frac{D}{100} \cdot \frac{N}{360}$$

$$\text{cost} = T - \text{discount}$$

where: T = total future value
D = discount rate
N = number of days to maturity

Example:

Canning Corporation purchases a $625,000 commercial paper due in 60 days at 5.4%. What is the discount and the cost?

Run:

```
Discount Commercial paper

Future value: $625000
Discount rate: (%) 5.4
Days to maturity: 60

Discount = $ 5625.00
    cost = $ 619375.

Would you like another run? (y/n) n
```

Program Listing:

```
program CommercialPaper(input, output);
var
  days: integer;
  value, rate, discount: real;

{$I ReadInt}
{$I NotAgain}

begin { main }
  writeln('Discount Commercial paper');
  repeat
    writeln;
    write('Future value: $');
    readln(value);
    write('Discount rate: (%) ');
    readln(rate);
```

```
    rate := rate / 100; { percent -> fraction }
    repeat
      write('Days to maturity: ')
    until ReadInt(days, 1, maxint);
    writeln;
    discount := value * rate * (days / 360);
    writeln('Discount = $', discount:7:2);
    writeln('    cost = $', value - discount:7:2);
    writeln
  until NotAgain
end.
```

14
Principal on a Loan

This program calculates the principal on a loan if you provide the interest rate, the amount of the regular payments, the number of payments per year, and the term of the loan. The principal is the original amount borrowed.

The principal calculation is based on the formula

$$P = \frac{R \cdot N}{i} \cdot \left(1 - \frac{1}{(1 + i/N)^{N \cdot Y}} \right)$$

where: P = principal
R = regular payment
i = annual interest rate
N = number of payments per year
Y = number of years

Examples:

Elizabeth has agreed to pay $250 bimonthly for three years to repay a loan with 20% interest. What was the amount of the loan?

Zoe can afford to make monthly payments of $180. If the loan company charges 16% interest, and Zoe can pay for 4 ½ years, what is the maximum amount she can borrow?

Run:

```
Principal on a Loan

Regular payment: $250
Number of payments per year? 6
Number of whole years: 3
Number of payments beyond last whole year: 0
Annual interest rate: (%) 20
Principal =   3343.45

Would you like another run? (y/n) y

Regular payment: $180
Number of payments per year? 12
Number of whole years: 4
Number of payments beyond last whole year: 6
Annual interest rate: (%) 16
Principal =   6897.49

Would you like another run? (y/n) n
```

Program Listing:

```
program LoanPrincipal(input, output);
var
  NumPays, NumYears, ExtraPays: integer;
  amount, percent, rate: real;

{$I ReadInt}
{$I IntRaise}
{$I NotAgain}

begin { main }
  writeln('Principal on a Loan');
  repeat
    writeln;
    write('Regular payment: $');
    readln(amount);
    repeat
      write('Number of payments per year? ')
    until ReadInt(NumPays, 1, maxint);
    repeat
      write('Number of whole years: ')
    until ReadInt(NumYears, 0, maxint);
    repeat
      write('Number of payments beyond last whole year: ')
    until ReadInt(ExtraPays, 0, maxint);
    write('Annual interest rate: (%) ');
    readln(percent);
    rate := percent / NumPays / 100;
    writeln('Principal = ', amount / rate
            * (1 - 1/IntRaise(rate + 1,
            NumPays * NumYears + ExtraPays)):6:2);
    writeln
  until NotAgain
end.
```

15
Regular Payments on a Loan

This program calculates the regular payment amount required to repay a loan over a specified time period. You must know the amount of the principal, the interest rate, the number of payments made per year, and the term. All payments, including the final payment, are equal.

The calculation is based on the formula

$$R = \frac{i \cdot P/N}{1 - \left(\frac{i}{N} + 1\right)^{-N \cdot Y}}$$

where: R = regular payment
i = annual interest rate
P = principal
N = number of payments per year
Y = number of years

Examples:

What regular payment must Nicole make on a loan of $4000 at 8% interest if her payments are quarterly for five years?

If Eric borrows $6500 from Maritime Savings and Loan and plans to take five years and six months to repay, what will his monthly payment be?

Run:

```
Regular Payment on a Loan

Principal: $4000
Number of payments per year? 4
Whole number of years: 5
Number of payments beyond last whole year: 0
Annual interest rate: (%) 8
Regular payment = $ 244.63

Would you like another run? (y/n) y

Principal: $6500
Number of payments per year? 12
Whole number of years: 5
Number of payments beyond last whole year: 6
Annual interest rate: (%) 12.5
Regular payment = $ 136.68

Would you like another run? (y/n) n
```

Program Listing:

```
program RegPayLoan(input, output);
var
   NumPays, NumYears, ExtraPays: integer;
   principal, percent, rate: real;

{$I ReadInt}
{$I IntRaise}
{$I NotAgain}

begin { main }
   writeln('Regular Payment on a Loan');
   repeat
     writeln;
     write('Principal: $');
     readln(principal);
     repeat
       write('Number of payments per year? ')
     until ReadInt(NumPays, 1, maxint);
     repeat
       write('Whole number of years: ')
     until ReadInt(NumYears, 0, maxint);
     repeat
       write('Number of payments beyond last whole year: ')
     until ReadInt(ExtraPays, 0, maxint);
     write('Annual interest rate: (%) ');
     readln(percent);
     rate := percent / NumPays / 100;
     writeln('Regular payment = $', principal * rate
             / (1 - IntRaise(rate + 1, - NumPays
             * NumYears - ExtraPays)):6:2);
     writeln
   until NotAgain
end.
```

16
Last Payment on a Loan

This program calculates the amount of the final payment on a loan, which will completely amortize the loan at the end of its term. You must know the principal, the amount of the regular payment, the interest rate, the number of payments per year, and the term of the loan.

The amount of the last payment normally differs from the amount of the regular payment. If the final payment is greater than the amount of the regular payment, it is called a "balloon payment." A balloon payment comes about when applying the regular payment to the remaining balance leaves a remainder that is less than another regular payment. In this case, the regular payment and the remainder are added together and the resulting final payment pays off the loan.

The amount of the final payment may also be less than the regular payment. If payment of the regular amount would result in a negative loan balance, the final payment is calculated by subtracting this negative loan balance from the regular payment. Thus, the last payment is less than the regular payment.

Calculations are based on the formula

$$\text{amount of last payment} = \text{regular payment} + \text{hypothetical balance due on a loan after } N \cdot Y \text{ regular payments}$$

where: N = number of payments per year
Y = number of years

Examples:

Manny borrowed $6000 at 5% for college expenses. If he pays $1000 annually for seven years, what will the final payment be?

Kate borrows $1150 at 8% interest, with a repayment schedule of $75 per month. One year and two months later, Kate wants to visit Europe for several months. How much must she pay in order to completely pay off her loan?

Run:

```
Last Payment on a Loan

Regular payment: $1000
Principal: $6000
Number of payments per year? 1
Number of whole years: 7
Number of payments beyond last whole year: 0
Annual interest rate: (%) 5
Last payment = $ 1300.59

Would you like another run? (y/n) y

Regular payment: $75
Principal: $1150
Number of payments per year? 12
Number of whole years: 1
Number of payments beyond last whole year: 2
Annual interest rate: (%) 8
Last payment = $ 240.37

Would you like another run? (y/n) n
```

Program Listing:

```pascal
program LastLoanPayment(input, output);
var
   NumPays, NumYears, ExtraPays, period: integer;
   principal, RegPay, percent, rate, balance: real;

{$I ReadInt}
{$I NotAgain}

begin { main }
   writeln('Last Payment on a Loan');
   repeat
     writeln;
     write('Regular payment: $');
     readln(RegPay);
     write('Principal: $');
     readln(principal);
     repeat
       write('Number of payments per year? ')
     until ReadInt(NumPays, 1, maxint);
     repeat
       write('Number of whole years: ')
     until ReadInt(NumYears, 0, maxint);
     repeat
       write('Number of payments beyond last whole year: ')
     until ReadInt(ExtraPays, 0, maxint);
     write('Annual interest rate: (%) ');
     readln(percent);
     rate := percent / NumPays / 100;
     balance := principal;
     for period := 1 to NumPays * NumYears + ExtraPays do
       balance := balance - (RegPay - balance * rate);
     writeln('Last payment = $', RegPay + balance:6:2);
     writeln
   until NotAgain
end.
```

17
Remaining Balance on a Loan

This program calculates the balance remaining on a loan after a specified number of payments. You must know the amount of the regular payment, the number of payments per year, the amount of the principal, the annual interest rate, and the number of the last payment made.

The remaining balance is calculated by the formula

$$\begin{matrix} \text{remaining} \\ \text{balance} \end{matrix} = \text{principal} - \begin{matrix} \text{amount amortized after} \\ N \cdot (Y - 1) + NI \text{ payments} \end{matrix}$$

where: N = number of payments per year
Y = year to calculate remaining balance
NI = payment number in year Y to calculate remaining balance

Example:

Kristien has borrowed $8000 at 17.2% interest. Her regular payment is $200 per month. If she has paid through the tenth payment in the fourth year, how much more does Kris owe on her loan?

Run:

```
Remaining Balance on a Loan

Regular payment: $200
Principal: $8000
Number of payments per year? 12
Annual interest rate: (%) 17.2
Year of last payment: (1 if 1st, etc.) 4
Number of payments made in last year: 10

Remaining balance = $ 2496.16

Would you like another run? (y/n) n
```

Program Listing:

```
program RemainingBalance(input, output);
var
  NumPays, YearNum, PayNum, period: integer;
  principal, RegPay, percent, rate, balance: real;

{$I ReadInt}
{$I NotAgain}

begin { main }
  writeln('Remaining Balance on a Loan');
  repeat
    writeln;
    write('Regular payment: $');
    readln(RegPay);
    write('Principal: $');
```

```
      readln(principal);
      repeat
        write('Number of payments per year? ')
      until ReadInt(NumPays, 1, maxint);
      write('Annual interest rate: (%) ');
      readln(percent);
      repeat
        write('Year of last payment: (1 if 1st, etc.) ')
      until ReadInt(YearNum, 1, maxint);
      repeat
        write('Number of payments made in last year: ')
      until ReadInt(PayNum, 0, maxint);
      writeln;
      rate := percent / NumPays / 100;
      balance := principal;
      for period := 1 to NumPays * (YearNum - 1) + PayNum do
        balance := balance - (RegPay - balance * rate);
      writeln('Remaining balance = $', balance:6:2);
      writeln
  until NotAgain
end.
```

18
Term of a Loan

This program calculates the amount of time needed to repay a loan. You must know the amount of the loan, the amount of the regular payment, the number of payments made per year, and the annual interest rate on the loan. All payments are equal.

The term of payment is derived from the formula

$$Y = - \frac{ln\left(1 - \dfrac{P \cdot i}{N \cdot R}\right)}{ln\left(1 + \dfrac{i}{N}\right)} \cdot \frac{1}{N}$$

where: Y = term of payments, in years
P = principal
i = annual interest rate
N = number of payments per year
R = amount of payments
ln = the natural logarithm

Examples:

What is the term of Nita and Kwang's mortgage, if the principal is $20,000, the interest rate is 18%, and payments are quarterly at $1000?

Emily borrows $12,669.00 at 16.8% interest. Her payments are $512.34 every two months. What is the term of her loan?

Run:

```
Term of a Loan

Regular payment: $1000
Principal: $20000
Number of payments per year? 4
Annual interest rate: (%) 18

Term = 13 years and 1 months.

Would you like another run? (y/n) y

Regular payment: $512.34
Principal: $12669
Number of payments per year? 6
Annual interest rate: (%) 16.8

Term = 7 years and 1 months.

Would you like another run? (y/n) n
```

38

Program Listing:

```
program TermLoan(input, output);
uses transcendentals; { omit this line if not using Apple Pascal }
var
   NumPays: integer;
   RegPay, principal, percent, rate, TermInYears: real;

{$I ReadInt}
{$I NotAgain}

begin { main }
   writeln('Term of a Loan');
   repeat
     writeln;
     write('Regular payment: $');
     readln(RegPay);
     write('Principal: $');
     readln(principal);
     repeat
        write('Number of payments per year? ')
     until ReadInt(NumPays, 1, maxint);
     write('Annual interest rate: (%) ');
     readln(percent);
     rate := percent / NumPays / 100;
     TermInYears:= -ln(1-(principal*rate/RegPay))/ln(1+rate)*(1/NumPays);
     writeln;
     write('Term = ', trunc(TermInYears),' years and ');
     writeln(round((TermInYears-trunc(TermInYears))*12), ' months.');
     writeln;
   until NotAgain
end.
```

19
Annual Interest Rate on a Loan

This program calculates the annual interest rate on a loan. You must know the amount of the principal, the amount of the regular payment, the number of payments per year, and the term of the loan.

The annual interest rate calculation uses the following method of approximation:

1. Guess an interest rate.

2. Compute the regular payment using the guessed rate.

$$R_1 = \frac{i \cdot P/N}{1 - (1 + i/N)^{-N \cdot Y}}$$

Round off R_1.

3. If the computed payment equals the actual payment, then the current guess is the approximate interest rate, and you have the answer.

4. Otherwise, save the current guess (we'll call it the previous interest rate) and calculate a new guess.

$$i_2 = i$$

$$i = i \pm |(i - i_2)/2| \quad \begin{cases} + \text{ if } R_1 < R \\ - \text{ if } R_1 > R \end{cases}$$

5. Return to step 2 and continue until a solution is found.

where:
i	=	interest rate
i_2	=	previous interest rate
R	=	input regular payment
R_1	=	computed regular payment
P	=	principal
N	=	number of payments per year
Y	=	number of years

Examples:

Deborah borrowed $3000 from her friend Noel with a written agreement to pay back $400 quarterly for two years. What is the interest rate?

Deirdre borrowed $10,000 to finance her medical school costs. She will make monthly payments of $120 for 9 ½ years. What is the interest rate?

Run:

```
Annual Interest Rate on a Loan

Regular payment: $400
Number of whole years: 2
Number of payments since last whole year: 0
Principal: $3000
Number of payments per year? 4

Annual interest rate =  5.83
```

Would you like another run? (y/n) y

Regular payment: $120
Number of whole years: 9
Number of payments since last whole year: 6
Principal: $10000
Number of payments per year? 12

Annual interest rate = 6.93

Would you like another run? (y/n) n

Program Listing:

```
program AnnualLoanIntRate(input, output);
var
   stop: boolean;
   NumPays, NumYears, ExtraPays: integer;
   LowGuess, HighGuess, GuessRate, GuessPay, RegPay, principal: real;

{$I ReadInt}
{$I IntRaise}
{$I RealTrunc}
{$I RealRound}
{$I NotAgain}

begin { main }
   writeln('Annual Interest Rate on a Loan');
   repeat
     writeln;
     write('Regular payment: $');
     readln(RegPay);
     repeat
       write('Number of whole years: ')
     until ReadInt(NumYears, 0, maxint);
     repeat
       write('Number of payments since last whole year: ')
     until ReadInt(ExtraPays, 0, maxint);
     write('Principal: $');
     readln(principal);
     principal := RealRound(principal, 2);
     repeat
       write('Number of payments per year? ')
     until ReadInt(NumPays, 1, maxint);
     writeln;
     LowGuess := 0.0;
     HighGuess := 1.0;
     stop := false;
     repeat
       { The true value must be between LowGuess and
         HighGuess, inclusive. }
       GuessRate := (LowGuess + HighGuess) / 2;
       GuessPay := GuessRate * principal
             / (1 - IntRaise(GuessRate + 1, - NumPays
             * NumYears - ExtraPays));
```

```
        if RealRound(GuessPay, 2) = RegPay then
          stop := true
        else if GuessPay < RegPay then
          LowGuess := GuessRate
          else
            HighGuess := GuessRate
      until stop;
      writeln('Annual interest rate = ', GuessRate * NumPays * 100:5:2);
      writeln;
  until NotAgain
end.
```

20
Mortgage Amortization Table

This program calculates and prints a loan repayment schedule including payment number, the amount of each payment that is applied as interest, the amount of the loan amortized with each payment, the balance remaining on the principal after each payment, the accumulated interest paid after each payment, and the amount of the last payment. The yearly totals of interest paid and amount of principal amortized are also printed. You must supply the amount of the regular payment, the term of payment, the number of payments per year, the amount of the principal, and the annual interest rate.

The schedule is calculated from the following formulas:

1. Payment number = payment number within each year

2. Amount of each payment paid as interest = remaining balance $\cdot i/N$

   where: i = annual interest rate
   N = number of payments per year

3. Amount amortized with each payment = $R - I$

   where: R = amount of regular payment
   I = amount of each payment paid as interest

4. Balance remaining = $P - \Sigma A$

   where: P = principal
   ΣA = sum of amounts amortized with each
   payment to date

5. Accumulated interest = ΣI

   where: ΣI = sum of amounts of each payment
   paid as interest to date

6. Amount of last payment = $R + (P - R \cdot N \cdot Y)$

   where: R = regular payment
   P = principal
   N = number of payments per year
   Y = number of years

Please note that this program will ask you for the number of years of amortization that you wish displayed, and you must round up to the next highest whole year. If you wish to see two years and six months displayed, you should request three years, as in the example below.

Example:

Phil needs $2100 to pay off some debts. His sister Ruth offers him the money at 6% interest. With payments of $75 monthly for two years and six months, what is Phil's repayment schedule?

Run:

```
Mortgage Amortization Table

Principal: $2100
Number of payments per year? 12
Number of years, including incomplete year: 3
Number of payments in last year: 6
Regular payment: $75
```

Annual interest rate: (%) 6

```
                 Mortgage Amortization Table
            Principal is $  2100.00 at   6.00% for 3 years.
            (Last Year contains only 6 payments)
               Regular Payment = $     75.00

    No.      Interest    Amortized     Balance   Accum Interest
     1        10.50        64.50       2035.50        10.50
     2        10.18        64.82       1970.68        20.68
     3         9.85        65.15       1905.53        30.53
     4         9.53        65.47       1840.06        40.06
     5         9.20        65.80       1774.26        49.26
     6         8.87        66.13       1708.13        58.13
     7         8.54        66.46       1641.67        66.67
     8         8.21        66.79       1574.88        74.88
     9         7.87        67.13       1507.75        82.75
    10         7.54        67.46       1440.29        90.29
    11         7.20        67.80       1372.49        97.49
    12         6.86        68.14       1304.35       104.35

 yr. 1       104.35       795.65


    No.      Interest    Amortized     Balance   Accum Interest
     1         6.52        68.48       1235.87       110.87
     2         6.18        68.82       1167.05       117.05
     3         5.84        69.16       1097.89       122.89
     4         5.49        69.51       1028.38       128.38
     5         5.14        69.86        958.52       133.52
     6         4.79        70.21        888.31       138.31
     7         4.44        70.56        817.75       142.75
     8         4.09        70.91        746.84       146.84
     9         3.73        71.27        675.57       150.57
    10         3.38        71.62        603.95       153.95
    11         3.02        71.98        531.97       156.97
    12         2.66        72.34        459.63       159.63

 yr. 2        55.28       844.72


    No.      Interest    Amortized     Balance   Accum Interest
     1         2.30        72.70        386.93       161.93
     2         1.93        73.07        313.86       163.86
     3         1.57        73.43        240.43       165.43
     4         1.20        73.80        166.63       166.63
     5         0.83        74.17         92.46       167.46
     6         0.46        92.46          0.00       167.92
          Last payment = $        92.92

 yr. 3         8.29       459.63
```

Would you like another run? (y/n) n

Program Listing:

```pascal
program MortgageAmortization(input, output);
const
   MaxLine = 23;
var
   LineNum, PaysPerYear, NumYears, LastPays, year: integer;
   balance, AccumInt, principal, RegPay, percent, rate: real;

{$I ReadInt}
{$I IntRaise}
{$I RealTrunc}
{$I RealRound}
{$I NotAgain}

   procedure ShowYear(NumPays: integer; LastYear: boolean);
   var
      period: integer;
      LastPay, SumInt, SumAmort: real;

      procedure ShowPeriod(pay: real);
      var
         interest, amortized: real;
      begin
         interest := RealRound(balance * rate, 2);
         AccumInt := AccumInt + interest;
         SumInt := SumInt + interest;
         amortized := pay - interest;
         SumAmort := SumAmort + amortized;
         balance := balance - amortized;
         writeln(period:5, interest:12:2,
                 amortized:12:2, balance:12:2, AccumInt:12:2)
      end; { ShowPeriod }

   begin { ShowYear }
      SumInt := 0;
      SumAmort := 0;
      LineNum := LineNum + NumPays + 4;
      if LineNum > MaxLine then
         begin
            page(output);
            LineNum := 0
         end;
      writeln('No.':5, 'Interest':12, 'Amortized':12, 'Balance':12,
              'Accum Interest':16);
      for period := 1 to NumPays do
         ShowPeriod(RegPay);
      if LastYear then
         begin
            period := NumPays + 1;
            LastPay := balance + RealRound(rate * balance, 2);
            ShowPeriod(LastPay);
            writeln('      Last payment = $', LastPay:12:2)
         end;
      writeln;
      writeln('yr.', year:2, SumInt:12:2, SumAmort:12:2);
      writeln;
      LineNum := LineNum + NumPays + 4
   end; { ShowYear }
```

```
    begin { main }
    writeln('Mortgage Amortization Table');
  repeat
    writeln;
    write('Principal: $');
    readln(principal);
    repeat
      write('Number of payments per year? ')
    until ReadInt(PaysPerYear, 1, maxint);
    repeat
      write('Number of years, including incomplete year: ')
    until ReadInt(NumYears, 1, maxint);
    repeat
      write('Number of payments in last year: ')
    until ReadInt(LastPays, 1, maxint);
    write('Regular payment: $');
    readln(RegPay);
    write('Annual interest rate: (%) ');
    readln(percent);
    rate := percent / PaysPerYear / 100;
    page(output);
    writeln('              Mortgage Amortization Table');
    writeln('        Principal is $', principal:9:2, ' at ', percent:5:2,
            '% for ', NumYears:0, ' years.');
    if LastPays = PaysPerYear then
      LineNum := 4
    else
      begin
        writeln('        (Last Year contains only ',LastPays:0, ' payments)');
        LineNum := 5
      end;
    writeln('              Regular Payment = $', RegPay:9:2);
    writeln;
    balance := principal;
    AccumInt := 0;
    for year := 1 to NumYears - 1 do
      ShowYear(PaysPerYear, false);
    year := NumYears;
    ShowYear(LastPays - 1, true);
    page(output)
  until NotAgain
end.
```

21
Greatest Common Divisor

This program calculates the greatest common divisor of two integers, based on the Euclidean algorithm.

Examples:

Find the greatest common divisor of 50 and 18.
    What is the greatest common divisor of 115 and 150?

Run:

```
Greatest Common Divisor

1st number (1 .. 32767) = 50
2nd number (1 .. 32767) = 18
GCD(50,18) = 2

Would you like another run? (y/n) y
1st number (1 .. 32767) = 115
2nd number (1 .. 32767) = 150
GCD(115,150) = 5

Would you like another run? (y/n) n
```

Program Listing:

```
program GreatestCommonDivisor(input, output);
type
  natural = 1..maxint;
var
  a, b: integer;

{$I ReadInt}
{$I NotAgain}

  function GCD(a, b: natural): integer;
  begin
    if a = b then
      GCD := a
    else if a > b then
      GCD := GCD(a - b, b)
    else
      GCD := GCD(a, b - a)
  end;

begin { main }
  writeln('Greatest Common Divisor');
  writeln;
  repeat
    write('1st number (1 .. ', maxint:0, ') = ');
    while not ReadInt(a, 1, maxint) do
      write('Invalid number, 1st number = ');
```

```
      write('2nd number (1 .. ', maxint: 0, ') = ');
      while not ReadInt(b, 1, maxint) do
        write('Invalid number, 2nd number = ');
      writeln('GCD(', a:0, ',', b:0, ') = ', GCD(a, b):0);
      writeln
    until NotAgain
end.
```

22
Prime Factors of Integers

This program lists the prime factors of any integer except zero. The factors are expressed in exponential notation.

In the second example below, the prime factors of 92 are 1, 2, and 23, with the additional non-prime factor of 4.

Examples:

What are the prime factors of −49?
    Factor 92 into primes.

Run:

```
Prime Factors of Integers

integer (0 ends program) = -49
-1
7 ^ 2
integer (0 ends program) = 92
1
2 ^ 2
23
integer (0 ends program) = 0
```

Program Listing:

```
program PrimeFactors(input, output);
var
  i: integer;
  factor: integer;

  procedure try(var i: integer; f: integer);
  var
    exponent: integer;
  begin
    if i mod f = 0 then
      begin
        write(f:0);
        exponent := 0;
        repeat
          i := i div f;
          exponent := exponent + 1
        until i mod f <> 0;
        if exponent > 1 then
          write(' ^ ', exponent:0);
        writeln
      end
  end; { try }
```

```
begin { main }
  writeln('Prime Factors of Integers');
  writeln;
  write('integer (0 ends program) = ');

  readln(i);
  while i <> 0 do
    begin
      if i < 0 then
        begin
          write('-');
          i := -i
        end;
      writeln('1');
      try(i, 2);
      factor := 3;
      while factor <= i div 2 do
        begin
          try(i, factor);
          factor := factor + 2
        end;
      if i <> 1 then { i is prime }
        writeln(i:0);
      write('integer (0 ends program) = ');
      readln(i)
    end
end.
```

23
Area of a Polygon

This program calculates the area of a polygon. You must supply the x coordinate and y coordinate of each vertex, and the coordinates must be entered in order of successive vertices.

The formula used to calculate the area is

$$\text{Area} = [(x_1 + x_2) \cdot (y_1 - y_2) + (x_2 + x_3) \cdot (y_2 - y_3) + \dots (x_n + x_1) \cdot (y_n - y_1)]/2$$

where: n = the number of vertices

Example:

Calculate the area of Lake Boyer.

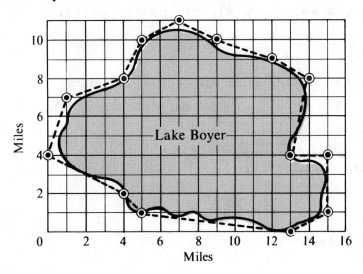

Run:

```
Area of a Polygon

Number of vertices: 14
x1: 0
y1: 4
x2: 1
y2: 7
x3: 4
y3: 8
x4: 5
y4: 10
x5: 7
y5: 11
x6: 9
y6: 10
x7: 12
y7: 9
x8: 14
y8: 8
x9: 13
```

```
y9: 4
x10: 15
y10: 4
x11: 15
y11: 1
x12: 13
y12: 0
x13: 5
y13: 1
x14: 4
y14: 2


Area =   108.0

Would you like another run? (y/n) n
```

Program Listing:

```pascal
program PolygonArea(input, output);
var
   NumVertices, vertex, area, x, y, x1, y1, LastX, LastY: integer;

{$I ReadInt}
{$I NotAgain}

   function GetVal(letter: char; num: integer): integer;
   var
     val: integer;
   begin
     repeat
       write(letter:1, num:0, ': ');
     until ReadInt(val, 0, maxint);
     GetVal := val
   end; { ReadVal }

begin { main }
  writeln('Area of a Polygon');
  repeat
    writeln;
    repeat
      write('Number of vertices: ')
    until ReadInt(NumVertices, 2, maxint);
    area := 0;
    x1 := GetVal('x', 1);
    y1 := GetVal('y', 1);
    LastX := x1;
    LastY := y1;
    for vertex := 2 to NumVertices do
      begin
        x := GetVal('x', vertex);
        y := GetVal('y', vertex);
        area := area + (LastX + x) * (LastY - y);
        LastX := x;
        LastY := y
      end;
    area := area + (LastX + x1) * (LastY - y1);
    writeln;
    writeln('Area = ', abs(area) / 2:6:1);
    writeln
  until NotAgain
end.
```

24
Parts of a Triangle

This program calculates three unknown parts of a triangle if three are known. At least one of the knowns must be the length of a side. The five possibilities for the known items are

1. Angle, side, angle
2. Side, angle, side
3. Angle, angle, side
4. Side, side, angle
5. Side, side, side

You may provide angles in either degrees or radians. If you provide the angles in degrees, you must convert degrees into a real number (that is, 5.3° rather than 20 degrees 15 minutes 2 seconds).

You must provide the known information in the order it appears in the triangle, either clockwise or counterclockwise.

Examples:

The base of a triangle measures 14 inches. The base angles are 0.45 and 2.1 radians. What are the measurements of the triangle?

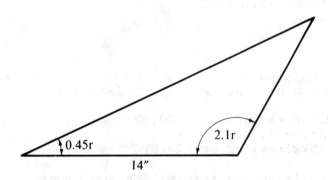

A square measures 8.76 inches × 8.76 inches. What is the length of the diagonal?

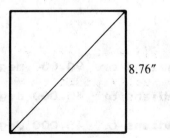

The ladder of a slide measures 10 feet, the slide 14 feet, and there are 13 feet of ground from the base of the ladder to the tip of the slide. How steep is the slide in degrees? In radians?

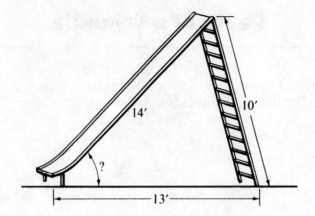

Run:

```
Parts of a Triangle

Choose the option specifying the information you have:

1) Angle, Side, Angle      4) Side, Side, Angle
2) Side, Angle, Side       5) Side, Side, Side
3) Angle, Angle, Side      6) END PROGRAM


1
Is angle in degrees?(y/n): n
Angle: .45
Side: 14
Is angle in degrees?(y/n): n
Angle: 2.1


Side 1 =   10.919
Opposite angle =     0.450 radians or   25.783 degrees.
Side 2 =   21.670
Opposite angle =     2.100 radians or  120.321 degrees.
Side 3 =   14.000
Opposite angle =     0.592 radians or   33.896 degrees.

Choose the option specifying the information you have:

1) Angle, Side, Angle      4) Side, Side, Angle
2) Side, Angle, Side       5) Side, Side, Side
3) Angle, Angle, Side      6) END PROGRAM


2
Side: 8.76
Is angle in degrees?(y/n): y
Angle: 90
Side: 8.76


Side 1 =   12.389
Opposite angle =     1.571 radians or   90.000 degrees.
Side 2 =    8.760
Opposite angle =     0.785 radians or   45.000 degrees.
Side 3 =    8.760
Opposite angle =     0.785 radians or   45.000 degrees.
```

```
Choose the option specifying the information you have:

1) Angle, Side, Angle    4) Side, Side, Angle
2) Side, Angle, Side     5) Side, Side, Side
3) Angle, Angle, Side    6) END PROGRAM

5
Side: 10
Side: 13
Side: 14

Side 1 =  10.000
Opposite angle =    0.755 radians or   43.279 degrees.
Side 2 =  13.000
Opposite angle =    1.100 radians or   63.027 degrees.
Side 3 =  14.000
Opposite angle =    1.286 radians or   73.694 degrees.


Choose the option specifying the information you have:

1) Angle, Side, Angle    4) Side, Side, Angle
2) Side, Angle, Side     5) Side, Side, Side
3) Angle, Angle, Side    6) END PROGRAM

6
```

Program Listing:

```pascal
program triangle(input, output);
uses transcendentals: { omit this line if not using Apple Pascal}
const
   pi = 3.14159265358979;
   ConvertFactor=0.0174532927;
type
   CharSet = set of char;
var
   stop, NoSoln: boolean;
   a1, a2, a3, s1, s2, s3: real;
{$I YesNotNo}
{$I read1char}
{$I arctan} { if your system misspells arctan as atan }
{$I arccos}
{$I arcsin}

   function GetSide: real;
   var s: real;
   begin
     write('Side: ');
     readln(s);
     GetSide := s
   end;

   function GetAngle: real;
   var a: real;
       w:char;
       AngInDeg:boolean;
   begin
     write('Is angle in degrees?(y/n): ');
     AngInDeg:= YesNotNo;
     write('Angle: ');
```

```
    readln(a);
    if AngInDeg then
      GetAngle:= a * ConvertFactor {conversion to radians from degrees}
    else
      GetAngle := a;
end;

function asa(a1, s, a2: real): real;
begin
  asa := s * sin(a1) / sin(a2)
end;

function sss(s1,s2,s3:real):real;
begin
 if (s1 = 0) or (s3 = 0) then begin
      NoSoln:= true;
      sss:= 0
      end
 else
      sss:=arccos((sqr(s1)+sqr(s3)-sqr(s2))/(2*s1*s3));
end;


procedure ShowOptions;
begin
  writeln('Choose the option specifying the information you have:');
  writeln;
  writeln('1) Angle, Side, Angle      4) Side, Side, Angle');
  writeln('2) Side, Angle, Side       5) Side, Side, Side');
  writeln('3) Angle, Angle, Side      6) END PROGRAM');
  writeln
end; { ShowOptions }

procedure Parts;
begin
  case read1char(['1'..'6']) of
    '1': begin
           a1 := GetAngle;
           s3 := GetSide;
           a2 := GetAngle;
           a3 := pi - a1 - a2;
           s1 := asa(a1, s3, a3);
           s2 := asa(a2, s3, a3)
         end;
    '2': begin
           s3 := GetSide;
           a1 := GetAngle;
           s2 := GetSide;
           s1 := sqrt(sqr(s3) + sqr(s2) - 2 * s3 * s2 * cos(a1));
           a2 := sss(s1,s2,s3);
           a3 := pi - a1 - a2
         end;
    '3': begin
           a3 := GetAngle;
           a2 := GetAngle;
          .s3 := GetSide;
           a1 := pi - a3 - a2;
           s1 := asa(a1, s3, a3);
           s2 := asa(a2, s3, a3)
         end;
```

```
    '4': begin
            s1 := GetSide:
            s2 := GetSide:
            a1 := GetAngle:
            if (cos(a1) <= 0) and (s1 <= s2) then
              NoSoln:= true
            else if s1 < s2 * sin(a1) then
              NoSoln := true
            else
              begin
                s3 := sqrt(sqr(s2) - sqr(s2 * sin(a1))):
                if s1 > s2 * sin(a1) then
                  s3 := s3 + sqrt(sqr(s1) + sqr(s2 * sin(a1))):
                a2 := sss(s1,s2,s3):
                a3:= pi - a1 - a2
              end
         end:
    '5': begin
            s1 := GetSide:
            s2 := GetSide:
            s3 := GetSide:
            a1 := arccos((sqr(s2) + sqr(s3) - sqr(s1)) / (2 * s2 * s3)):
            a2 := sss(s1,s2,s3):
            a3 := pi - a1 - a2
         end:
    '6': stop := true
end: { case }


begin { main }
  writeln('Parts of a Triangle'):
  stop := false:
  repeat
    writeln:
    ShowOptions:
    NoSoln := false:
    Parts:
    if not stop and not NoSoln then
      begin
        writeln:
        writeln('Side 1 = ', s1:7:3):
        write('Opposite angle = ', a1:7:3, ' radians or '):
        writeln(a1/ConvertFactor:7:3, ' degrees.'):
        writeln('Side 2 = ', s2:7:3):
        write('Opposite angle = ', a2:7:3, ' radians or '):
        writeln(a2/ConvertFactor:7:3,' degrees.'):
        writeln('Side 3 = ', s3:7:3):
        write('Opposite angle = ', a3:7:3, ' radians or '):
        writeln(a3/ConvertFactor:7:3,' degrees.'):
      end
  until stop
end.
```

25
Analysis of Two Vectors

This program calculates the angle between two given vectors, the angle between each vector and axis, and the magnitude of each vector. The vectors are given in three-dimensional space.

Example:

Find the angle (θ) between a diagonal of a cube and a diagonal of one of its faces. The cube measures $4 \times 4 \times 4$.

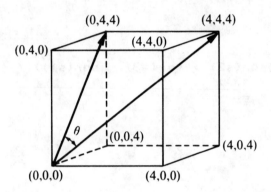

Run:

```
Analysis of Two Vectors

Input vector A:
X component: 0
Y component: 4
Z component: 4
Input vector B:
X component: 4
Y component: 4
Z component: 4

Vector A:
magnitude =  5.65685
Angle with X-axis =   90.0002
Angle with Y-axis =   45.0002
Angle with Z-axis =   45.0002

Vector B:
magnitude =  6.92820
Angle with X-axis =   54.7358
Angle with Y-axis =   54.7358
Angle with Z-axis =   54.7358

Angle between a and b =  35.2646

Would you like another run? (y/n) n
```

Program Listing:

```
program VectorAnalysis(input, output);
uses transcendentals; { omit this line if not using Apple Pascal }
const
  pi = 3.14159265358979;
type
{$I vectors}
var
  angle: real;
  a, b: vector;

{$I ReadReal}
{$I GetVector}
{$I Arctan}
{$I Arccos}
{$I NotAgain}

  function mag(v: vector): real;
  begin
    mag := sqrt(sqr(v.x) + sqr(v.y) + sqr(v.z))
  end;

  procedure describe(v: vector);
  var
    m: real;
  begin
    m := mag(v);
    writeln('magnitude = ', m);
    if m <> 0.0 then
      begin
        writeln('Angle with X-axis = ', arccos(v.x / m) * 180 / pi:9:5);
        writeln('Angle with Y-axis = ', arccos(v.y / m) * 180 / pi:9:5);
        writeln('Angle with Z-axis = ', arccos(v.z / m) * 180 / pi:9:5);
        writeln;
      end
  end; { describe }

begin { main }
  writeln('Analysis of Two Vectors');
  repeat
    writeln;
    writeln('Input vector A:');
    GetVector(a);
    writeln('Input vector B:');
    GetVector(b);
    writeln;
    writeln('Vector A:');
    describe(a);
    writeln('Vector B:');
    describe(b);
    angle := (a.x*b.x + a.y*b.y + a.z*b.z) / (mag(a) * mag(b));
    if angle = 0 then
      angle := 90.0
    else
      angle := arccos(angle) * 180 / pi;
    writeln('Angle between a and b = ', angle:9:5);
    writeln
  until NotAgain
end.
```

26
Operations on Two Vectors

This program performs addition, subtraction, scalar (dot) product, and cross-product calculation on two vectors in three-dimensional space.

Example:

Vectors are drawn from the origin to points A (5, −1, 2) and B (1, 4, 9). Add, subtract, and calculate the dot and cross-products of these two vectors.

Run:

```
Operations on Two Vectors

Input vector A:
X component: 5
Y component: -1
Z component: 2
Input vector B:
X component: 1
Y component: 4
Z component: 9

A + B: x =      6.000 y =      3.000 z =     11.000
A - B: x =      4.000 y =     -5.000 z =     -7.000
A . B:     19.000
A X B: x =    -17.000 y =    -43.000 z =     21.000

Would you like another run? (y/n) n
```

Program Listing:

```
program VectorOperations(input, output);
type
{$I vectors}
var
  a, b : vector;

{$I ReadReal}
{$I GetVector}
{$I NotAgain}

begin { main }
  writeln('Operations on Two Vectors');
  repeat
    writeln;
    writeln('Input vector A:');
    GetVector(a);
    writeln('Input vector B:');
    GetVector(b);
    writeln;
```

```
    writeln('A + B: x = ', a.x+b.x:9:3, ' y = ', a.y+b.y:9:3,
            ' z = ', a.z+b.z:9:3);
    writeln('A - B: x = ', a.x-b.x:9:3, ' y = ', a.y-b.y:9:3,
            ' z = ', a.z-b.z:9:3);
    writeln('A . B: ', a.x * b.x + a.y * b.y + a.z * b.z:9:3);
    writeln('A X B: x = ', a.y*b.z-a.z*b.y:9:3, ' y = ', a.z*b.x-a.x*b.z:9:3,
            ' z = ', a.x*b.y-a.y*b.x:9:3);
    writeln
  until NotAgain
end.
```

27
Angle Conversion: Radians to Degrees

This program converts an angle given in radians to degrees, minutes, and seconds.

Examples:

How many degrees, minutes, and seconds are there in an angle of 2.5 radians?
　An angle of 118 radians is how many degrees, minutes, and seconds?

Run:

```
Angle Conversion: Radians to Degrees

Angle in radians: 2.5
    Degrees = 143
    Minutes = 14
    Seconds =  22.0000

Would you like another run? (y/n) y

Angle in radians: 118
    Degrees = 280
    Minutes = 54
    Seconds =   3.56250

Would you like another run? (y/n) n
```

Program Listing:

```
program RadiansToDegrees(input,output);
const   pi = 3.14159265;
        TwoPi = 6.28318530;

var   angle : real;

{$I NotAgain }
{$I ReadReal }

procedure ReadInput;
begin
  repeat
    write('Angle in radians: ')
  until ReadReal(angle)
end; { procedure ReadInput }

function RealMod(a, b : real) : real;
begin
  while a >= b do
    a:= a - b;
  RealMod:= a
end;   { function RealMod }
```

ANGLE CONVERSION: RADIANS TO DEGREES

```
procedure Convert;
var  Degrees, Minutes : integer;
     Seconds : real;

begin
   angle:= RealMod(angle , TwoPi);
   Seconds:= 3600.0 * 180.0 * angle / pi;
   Degrees:= trunc(seconds / 3600);
   Seconds:= seconds - Degrees * 3600.0;
   Minutes:= trunc(seconds / 60);
   Seconds:= seconds - Minutes * 60.0;
   writeln('   Degrees = ', Degrees:3:5);
   writeln('   Minutes = ', Minutes:2:5);
   writeln('   Seconds = ', Seconds:2:5)
end; { procedure Convert }

begin  { main }
   writeln; writeln('Angle Conversion: Radians to Degrees');
   repeat
     writeln;
     ReadInput;
     Convert;
     writeln;
   until NotAgain
end.
```

28
Angle Conversion: Degrees to Radians

This program converts an angle given in degrees, minutes, and seconds to radians.

Examples:

An angle measures 30 degrees, 5 minutes, 3 seconds. What is the measure of this angle in radians?
  What is the measure in radians of an angle measuring 278 degrees, 19 minutes, 54 seconds? What is the measure in radians of an angle measuring 721 degrees, 0 minutes, 0 seconds?

Run:

```
Angle Conversion: Degrees to Radians

degrees minutes seconds = 30 5 3
Radians =   5.25067E-1

Would you like another run? (y/n) y
degrees minutes seconds = 278 19 54
Radians =   4.85780

Would you like another run? (y/n) y
degrees minutes seconds = 721 0 0
Radians =   1.74533E-2

Would you like another run? (y/n) n
```

Program Listing:

```
program DegToRad(input, output);
const
  pi = 3.14159;
var
  deg, min: integer;
  sec: real;

{$I NotAgain}

begin { main }
  writeln('Angle Conversion: Degrees to Radians');
  writeln;
  repeat
    write('degrees minutes seconds = ');
    readln(deg, min, sec);
    writeln('Radians = ',
            ((deg mod 360 * 60 + min) * 60.0 + sec) /3600 * pi /180);
    writeln
  until NotAgain
end.
```

29
Coordinate Conversion

This program converts the coordinates of a point given in Cartesian coordinates to polar coordinates, and vice versa.

The formulas for the conversions are

$$r = \sqrt{x^2 + y^2}$$

$$A = \text{arctangent } (y/x)$$

$$x = r \cdot \text{cosine } (A)$$

$$y = r \cdot \text{sine } (A)$$

where: x = abscissa $\Big\}$ Cartesian coordinates
$\quad\quad y$ = ordinate

$\quad\quad r$ = magnitude of ray $\Big\}$ Polar coordinates
$\quad\quad A$ = angle (in degrees)

Examples:

What are the Cartesian coordinates of the point (2, 30.5°)?

If a point is at (7, 18) in the Cartesian system, what are its polar coordinates?

A point is located at (0, −46.8). What are its polar coordinates?

Run:

```
Coordinate Conversion

C -> Cartesian to polar
P -> Polar to Cartesian
Q -> Quit
P

radius angle (in degrees) = 2 30.5
x =  1.723, y =  1.015

C -> Cartesian to polar
P -> Polar to Cartesian
Q -> Quit
c

X Y = 7 18
radius =  19.313, angle =  68.749 degrees.

C -> Cartesian to polar
P -> Polar to Cartesian
Q -> Quit
c

X Y = 0 -46.8
radius =  46.800, angle =  270.000 degrees.
```

```
C -> Cartesian to polar
P -> Polar to Cartesian
Q -> Quit
q
```

Program Listing:

```
program coords(input, output);
uses transcendentals; { Omit this line if not using Apple Pascal }
const
  pi = 3.14159265358979;
type
  CharSet = set of char;
var
  c: char;
  stop: boolean;
  x, y, radius, angle: real;

{$I arctan}
{$I read1char}

begin { main }
  writeln('Coordinate Conversion');
  stop := false;
  repeat
    writeln;
    writeln('C -> Cartesian to polar');
    writeln('P -> Polar to Cartesian');
    writeln('Q -> Quit');
    c := read1char(['c','p','q']);
    writeln;
    case c of
      'c': begin
              write('X Y = ');
              readln(x, y);
              if x = 0 then
                if y = 0 then
                  begin
                    radius := 0;
                    angle := 0
                  end
                else
                  begin
                    radius := abs(y);
                    if y > 0 then
                      angle := 90
                    else
                      angle := 270
                  end
              else
                if y = 0 then
                  begin
                    radius := abs(x);
                    if x >= 0 then
                      angle := 0
                    else
                      angle := 180
                  end
```

```
            else
              begin
                radius := sqrt(sqr(x) + sqr(y));
                angle := arctan(y/x) * 180 / pi
              end;
          writeln('radius = ', radius:6:3,
                  ', angle = ', angle:6:3, ' degrees.')
        end;
    'p': begin
          write('radius angle (in degrees) = ');
          readln(radius, angle);
          angle := angle * pi / 180;
          writeln('x = ', radius * cos(angle):6:3,
                  ', y = ', radius * sin(angle):6:3)
        end;
    'q': stop := true
    end { case }
  until stop
end.
```

30
Coordinate Plot

This program plots points on a set of coordinate axes. You must provide the x and y coordinates of all points to be plotted, the endpoints of the x and y axes, and the increment between points on each axis.

The graph is unconventional in that the x axis runs vertically while the y axis runs horizontally. Either turn your output 90° counterclockwise, or mentally adjust to the new convention. The point where the axes cross is printed at the top of each graph; it is not necessarily at (0,0).

Program Notes

The program is currently set up for output that prints no more than 70 columns. If you want to change this parameter, locate procedure ReadData and change the constant "maxscreen" to the new maximum width of the output device.

The program will accept no more than 100 points. To change this parameter, set the global constant "maxpoints" equal to the new maximum.

Example:

The heights of twelve men and their sons are recorded in the table below. Plot the data points.

Father	65	63	67	64	68	62	70	66	68	67	69	71
Son	68	66	68	65	69	66	68	65	71	67	68	70

Height in Inches

Run:

```
Coordinate Plot

X-Axis: Left Endpoint? 62
X-Axis: Right Endpoint? 73
X-Axis: Increment? .5
Y-Axis: Left Endpoint? 62
Y-Axis: Right Endpoint? 73
Y-Axis: Increment? .25
Please input the number of points 12
X-Coordinate of point 1 ? 65
Y-Coordinate of point 1 ? 68
X-Coordinate of point 2 ? 63
Y-Coordinate of point 2 ? 66
X-Coordinate of point 3 ? 67
Y-Coordinate of point 3 ? 68
X-Coordinate of point 4 ? 64
Y-Coordinate of point 4 ? 65
X-Coordinate of point 5 ? 68
Y-Coordinate of point 5 ? 69
X-Coordinate of point 6 ? 62
```

```
Y-Coordinate of point 6 ? 66
X-Coordinate of point 7 ? 70
Y-Coordinate of point 7 ? 68
X-Coordinate of point 8 ? 66
Y-Coordinate of point 8 ? 65
X-Coordinate of point 9 ? 68
Y-Coordinate of point 9 ? 71
X-Coordinate of point 10 ? 67
Y-Coordinate of point 10 ? 67
X-Coordinate of point 11 ? 69
Y-Coordinate of point 11 ? 68
X-Coordinate of point 12 ? 71
Y-Coordinate of point 12 ? 70
```

```
Itersection of Axes at (62 62)
***********************+*********************************Y
*
*
*                   +
*
*             +
*
*                      +
*
*             +
*
*                 +    +
*
*                        +        +
*
*                 +
*
*                 +
*
*                     +
*
*
*
*
*
```

Program Listing:

```pascal
program Plotcord (input,output);

const
 maxpoints=100;

type
 index=0..maxpoints;
 arraycord=array[index] of integer;

var
 XCord,YCord:arraycord;
 LastPoint:index;
 XLeft,XRight:integer;
 YLeft,YRight:integer;
 XInc,YInc:real;
 Current:integer;
```

69

```
{$I ReadInt}
procedure ReadData;
const
 maxscreen=70;
var
 i:index;
 X,Y:real;

begin
write('X-Axis: Left Endpoint? ');    {set up X-Axis}
readln(XLeft);
write('X-Axis: Right Endpoint? ');
readln(XRight);
write('X-Axis: Increment? ');
readln(XInc);
XRight:=round((XRight-XLeft)/XInc);
YRight:=maxscreen + 1;
while YRight > maxscreen do begin  {set up Y-Axis}
   write('Y-Axis: Left Endpoint? ');
   readln(YLeft);
   write('Y-Axis: Right Endpoint? ');
   readln(YRight);
   write('Y-Axis: Increment? ');
   readln(YInc);
   YRight:=round((YRight - YLeft)/YInc);
   if YRight > maxscreen then  {too big for screen?}
      writeln('Y-Range too large')
   end;  {while YRight ect.}
   repeat
      write('Please input the number of points ');
   until ReadInt (LastPoint,1,maxpoints);
for i:= 1 to LastPoint do begin  {read in all coordinates}
   write('X-Coordinate of point ',i,' ? ');
   readln(X);
   XCord[i]:=round((x-XLeft)/XInc);
   write('Y-Coordinate of point ',i,' ? ');
   readln(Y);
   YCord[i]:=round((y-YLeft)/YInc)
   end  {for LastPoint}
end;  {ReadData}


procedure Sort;
var
 X,Y:integer;
 i,j:index;


begin
for i:= 2 to LastPoint do begin
   Y:=YCord[i];
   X:=XCord[i];
   j:=i-1;
   while (X < XCord[j]) and (j<>0) do begin    {sort X's}
      YCord[j+1]:=YCord[j];
      XCord[j+1]:=XCord[j];
      j:=j-1
      end;  {while X ect}
   while (X = XCord[j]) and (Y < YCord[j]) and (j<>0) do begin
      YCord[j+1]:=YCord[j];
      XCord[j+1]:=XCord[j];
```

```
        j:=j-1
        end;
    XCord[j+1]:=X;
    YCord[j+1]:=Y
    end   {for LastPoint}
end;  {sort}


procedure Duplicate;
var
  Identical:boolean;

begin
Identical:=true;
while (Current<maxpoints) and (identical) do
  if (XCord[Current]=XCord[Current+1]) and (YCord[Current]=YCord[Current+1]) then
    Current:=Current+1
else
    Identical:=false
end;


procedure PrintGraph;
var
  i,j:integer;

begin
writeln;writeln('Intersection of Axes at (',XLeft:2,' ',YLeft:2,')');
Current:=1;
for i:= 0 to XRight do begin
    for j:= 0 to YRight do begin
        if (XCord[Current]=i) and (YCord[Current]=j) then begin
            write('+');
            if Current<maxpoints then begin
                Current:=Current+1;
                Duplicate
                end
            end
        else if (i=0) or (j=0) then
            write('*')
        else
            write(' ')
        end;
    if i=0 then
        write('Y');
    writeln
    end;
writeln('X')
end;


begin {MAIN}
writeln('Coordinate Plot');
writeln;
ReadData;
Sort;
PrintGraph;
end.   {MAIN}
```

31
Plot of Polar Equation

This program plots a given function in polar coordinates. There are up to 90 points plotted, one every four degrees. (Some points may overlap.)

The graph is conventional in that the x axis runs horizontally, the y axis runs vertically, and they intersect at zero. You need only specify the absolute value of the endpoints.

Program Notes

The increment between each point on the x and y axes is adjusted so that a value of 1 on either axis is equidistant from zero. This allows the function to be plotted with minimal distortion. An adjustment of each increment is necessary because of different spacing horizontally and vertically on an output device. This program assumes ten spaces per inch horizontally and six spaces per inch vertically. If your output device differs, the graph may be distorted. The constants "XPlot" and "YPlot" help control the output spacing. If you need to alter these constants, make a series of changes and observe the effects on your output. Then choose the constant values that give you the best results.

If you need to plot more than 90 points, you can change the constant "maxpoints" but you may overwhelm the capabilities of your output device.

You must enter the function that you want to see plotted. In the function "Plot" find the line that reads "Plot: = 2 * (1 − cos(Rad))". Your function must follow the "Plot:=" and it must be expressed in terms of "Rad" where "Rad" is the radius.

You should pause every few lines when you are printing the plot, to prevent the printer's buffer from overloading. A pause of a few seconds will allow the printer to print its contents and be ready for more coordinate data from the computer. If you generate a garbled plot, suspect an overloaded print buffer before you do other troubleshooting.

Example:

Plot the function $f(Rad) = 2 * (1 − cos(Rad))$.

Run:

```
Plot of Polar Equation
Absolute Value of Endpoints ? 4
Increment of X-Axis=  0.133333
Increment of Y-Axis=  0.222222
```

Program Listing:

```
program Polar(input,output);
uses transcend;  {omit if not Apple Pascal}

const
 maxpoints=90;
 XPlot=30;
 YPlot=18;

type
 index=0..maxpoints;
 polararray=array[index] of integer;

var
 XCord,YCord:polararray;
```

73

```pascal
Absolute:integer;
Current:index;


procedure ReadData;

begin
writeln('Plot of Polar Equation');
write('Absolute Value of Endpoints ? ');
readln(Absolute);
writeln('Increment of X-Axis= ',Absolute/XPlot:2:7);
writeln('Increment of Y-Axis= ',Absolute/YPlot:2:7);
end;   {ReadData}


function Plot(Rad:real):real;

begin
Plot:=2*(1 - cos(Rad))   {function to be plotted, can be changed}
end;     {function Plot}


procedure Calculate;
const
  convert=6.981317E-2;
var
  i:index;
  Rad:real;

begin
for i:= 1 to maxpoints do begin
    Rad:=convert * i;
    XCord[i]:=round((Plot(Rad)*cos(Rad)/Absolute)*XPlot);
    YCord[i]:=round((-Plot(Rad)*sin(Rad)/Absolute)*YPlot)
    end {for maxpoints}
end;     {Calculate}


procedure Sort;
var
  X,Y:integer;
  i,j:index;
  left,right,middle:index;

begin
for i:= 2 to maxpoints do begin
    Y:=YCord[i];
    X:=XCord[i];
    left:=1;
    right:=i-1;
    while left <= right do begin
        middle:=(left + right) div 2;
        if Y > YCord[middle] then
            right:=middle-1
        else
            left:=middle+1
        end;
    for j:=i-1 downto left do begin
```

```
        XCord[j+1]:=XCord[j];
        YCord[j+1]:=YCord[j]
        end;
    left:=left-1;
    while (Y = YCord[left]) and (X < XCord[left]) and (left<>0) do
        begin
            YCord[left+1]:=YCord[left];
            XCord[left+1]:=XCord[left];
            left:=left-1
        end;
        XCord[left+1]:=X;
        YCord[left+1]:=Y
    end  {for maxpoints}
end;  {sort}


procedure Duplicate;
var
  Identical:boolean;

begin
Identical:=true;
while (Current<maxpoints) and (Identical) do begin
    if (XCord[Current]=XCord[Current+1])
        and (YCord[Current]=YCord[Current+1]) then
            Current:=Current+1
    else
        Identical:=false
    end  {while Current etc}
end;  {Duplicate}


procedure PrintGraph;
var
  i,j,k:integer;

begin
Current:=1;
for i:= YPlot downto -YPlot do begin
    for j:= -XPlot to XPlot do begin
        if (i=YCord[Current]) and (j=XCord[Current]) then begin
            write('+');
            if Current < maxpoints then begin
                Current:=Current+1;
                Duplicate   {duplicate coordinates?}
                end
            end   {if YCord etc}
        else if (j=0) or (i=0) then
            write('*')
        else
            write(' ')
        end;  {for XPlot etc}
    if i=0 then    {print the X label}
        write('X');
    writeln
    end;  {for YPlot etc}
for k:=1 to XPlot do {print the Y label}
    write(' ');
writeln('Y')
end;  {PrintGraph}
```

```
begin   {MAIN}
ReadData;
Calculate;
Sort;
PrintGraph;
end.   {MAIN}
```

32
Plot of Functions

This program calculates and plots up to nine functions. All must be functions of x and all will be plotted on the same set of axes. To set up the axes, input the endpoints of the x and y axes and the increment for the points on each axis.

The graph is unconventional in that the x axis runs vertically while the y axis runs horizontally. Either turn your output 90° counterclockwise, or mentally adjust to the new convention. The point where the axes cross is printed at the top of each graph; it is not necessarily at (0,0).

Program Notes

The program is currently set up for output that prints no more than 70 columns. If you want to change this parameter, locate the REPEAT loop that includes the procedure called "GetYCoOrds." The next statements should include "If Upper Bound >70" and "Until Upper Bound <= 70". Change the 70 in each of these Pascal statements to whatever your maximum column width is.

You must write Pascal statements which define your functions. The first function assignment should be to the array element Funcs[1], the second function to Funcs[2], and so on. The equation must include the real variable "PlotPoint." If your first equation is $f(x) = cos(x)$, then *Funcs[1] := cos(PlotPoint)*. The examples show the functions *cos(PlotPoint)* and *sin(PlotPoint)*.

Example:

Plot the equations $f(x) = cos(x)$ and $f(x) = sin(x)$.

Run:

Plot of Functions

Please enter the number of functions to be plotted : 2
X-axis:left end point : -5
X-axis:right end point : 5
X-axis:increment : .25
Y-axis:lower end point : -2
Y-axis:upper end point : 2
Y-axis:increment : .1

X-axis crosses Y-axis at Y=-2
Y-axis crosses X-axis at X=-5

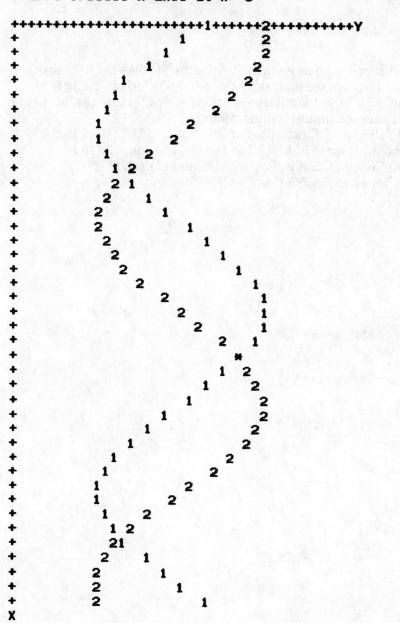

Program Listing:

```
program PlotOfFunctions(input,output);
uses transcend;   { Omit if not using Apple Pascal }
var   ch : char;
      NumOfFunc : integer;
      PlotNum,Hits : integer;
      i,j : integer;

      LowerXBound, UpperXBound : integer;
      PlotPoint, XIncrement : real;

      LowerYBound, UpperYBound : integer;
      Yincrement : real;
      Funcs : array [1..9] of real;

{$I ReadInt }
{$I ReadReal }


procedure GetXCoOrds;
begin
  repeat
    write('X-axis:left end point : ')
  until ReadInt(LowerXBound, -maxint, maxint);
  repeat
    write('X-axis:right end point : ')
  until ReadInt(UpperXBound, -maxint, maxint);
  repeat
    write('X-axis:increment : ')
  until ReadReal(XIncrement)
end;  { procedure GetXCoOrds }

procedure GetYCoOrds;
begin
  repeat
    write('Y-axis:lower end point : ')
  until ReadInt(LowerYBound, -maxint, maxint);
  repeat
    write('Y-axis:upper end point : ')
  until ReadInt(UpperYBound, -maxint, maxint);
  repeat
    write('Y-axis:increment : ')
  until ReadReal(YIncrement)
end; { procedure GetYCoOrds }

procedure PrintCord;
begin
for i := 0 to UpperYBound do
   begin
   Hits := 0;
   for j := 1 to NumOfFunc do
      begin
      if Funcs[j] = i then
        begin
        Hits := Hits + 1;
        PlotNum := j
        end
      end;
   if (PlotPoint = LowerXBound) or (i=0) then
      ch := '+'
```

79

```
      else ch := ' ';

      if Hits = 1 then
         ch := chr(PlotNum +ord('0'))
      else if Hits > 1 then ch := '*';
      write(ch)
      end
end;  {procedure PrintCord}


begin  { main }
   writeln('Plot of Functions');
   writeln;
   repeat
      write('Please enter the number of functions to be plotted : ');
   until ReadInt(NumOfFunc, 1, 2);
   GetXCoOrds;
   repeat
      GetYCoOrds;
      UpperYBound := round((UpperYBound - LowerYBound) / YIncrement);
      if UpperYBound > 70 then
         writeln('Y-range too large');
   until UpperYBound <= 70;
   writeln;
   writeln;
   writeln('X-axis crosses Y-axis at Y=',LowerYBound);
   writeln('Y-axis crosses X-axis at X=',LowerXBound);
   writeln;
   PlotPoint := LowerXBound;
   while PlotPoint <= UpperXBound do
      begin
         { Define your functions here }
         Funcs[1] := cos(PlotPoint);
         Funcs[2] := sin(PlotPoint);
         for i:= 1 to NumOfFunc do
            Funcs[i] := round((Funcs[i] -LowerYBound) / YIncrement);
         PrintCord;
         if PlotPoint <= LowerXBound then
             write('Y');
         writeln;
         PlotPoint := PlotPoint + XIncrement
         end;
      writeln('X')
end.
```

33

Linear Interpolation

This program calculates the y coordinates of points on a line, if the x coordinates are known. You must know the coordinates of at least two points on the line.

Each point is interpolated using the following formula:

$$y = y_1 + \frac{(y_2 - y_1) \cdot (x - x_1)}{(x_2 - x_1)}$$

where: $\quad x_1, y_1 = $ coordinates of first point on the line
$\quad\quad\quad\quad x_2, y_2 = $ coordinates of second point on the line
$\quad\quad\quad\quad\quad x = $ abscissa of point to be interpolated
$\quad\quad\quad\quad\quad y = $ ordinate of the point on the line with x

In addition to the obvious geometric applications, questions that use linear interpolation include
- Conversions from one measurement system (of temperature, weight, length, etc.) to another.

- Percents of dollar amounts. A percent may be thought of as a point whose y coordinate is 100 and whose x coordinate is the real number which precedes the % symbol. If you know a tax rate and a taxable amount, you can calculate the dollar amount of the tax, for example.

- Percents of any known quantity.

Examples:

A table of temperatures shows that 60°F is 15.56°C and 90°F is 32.22°C. What are the Celsius values of 73°F and 85.6°F?

A new sales tax of 17.5% has been enacted. What is the sales tax on a furniture purchase of $455.68?

Run:

```
Linear Interpolation

Enter point a:
  x: 60
  y: 15.56
Enter point b:
  x: 90
  y: 32.22
x for interpolation: 73
interpolated y =    22.779

Another point on this line? (y/n) y
x for interpolation: 85.6
interpolated y =    29.777

Another point on this line? (y/n) n
Would you like another run? (y/n) y

Enter point a:
  x: 0
  y: 0
```

```
Enter point b:
  x: 100
  y: 17.5
x for interpolation: 455.68
interpolated y =      79.744

Another point on this line? (y/n) n
Would you like another run? (y/n) n
```

Program Listing:

```pascal
program LinearInterpolation(input, output);
type
  CharSet = set of char;
{$I points}
var
  x, y: real;
  a, b: point;

{$I ReadReal}
{$I ReadPoint}
{$I read1char}
{$I NotAgain}

begin { main }
  writeln('Linear Interpolation');
  repeat
    writeln;
    writeln('Enter point a:');
    ReadPoint(a);
    writeln('Enter point b:');
    ReadPoint(b);
    repeat
      repeat
        write('x for interpolation: ')
      until ReadReal(x);
      y := a.y + (b.y - a.y) / (b.x - a.x) * (x - a.x);
      writeln('interpolated y = ', y:9:3);
      writeln;
      write('Another point on this line? (y/n) ')
    until read1char(['y', 'n']) = 'n'
  until NotAgain
end.
```

34
Curvilinear Interpolation

This program computes y coordinates of points on a curve given their x coordinates. You must input coordinates of known points on the curve, no two having the same abscissa.

The computations are performed using the Lagrange method of interpolation.

Program Notes

The program allows you to enter a maximum of 50 known points on a curve. Change the constant "maxpoints" if you want a higher or lower limit.

Examples:

Consider the curve $y = x^3 - 3x + 3$. You know that the points $(-3, -15)$, $(-2, 1)$, $(-1, 5)$, $(0, 3)$, $(1, 1)$, $(2, 5)$, and $(3, 21)$ are on the curve. What is the value of y when $x = -1.65$ and 0.2?

Given the following points from a sine curve, what is the sine of -2.47 and the sine of 1.5?

$(-5, 0.958)$	$(0, 0)$
$(-4, 0.757)$	$(1, 0.841)$
$(-3, -0.141)$	$(2, 0.909)$
$(-2, -0.909)$	$(3, 0.141)$
$(-1, -0.841)$	$(4, -0.757)$
	$(5, -0.959)$

Run:

```
Curvilinear Interpolation


Number of Known Points? 7
X of Point 1 ? -3
Y of Point 1 ? -15
X of Point 2 ? -2
Y of Point 2 ? 1
X of Point 3 ? -1
Y of Point 3 ? 5
X of Point 4 ? 0
Y of Point 4 ? 3
X of Point 5 ? 1
Y of Point 5 ? 1
X of Point 6 ? 2
Y of Point 6 ? 5
X of Point 7 ? 3
Y of Point 7 ? 21



Interpolate: X =? -1.65
             Y =   3.45788

Interpolate more points on same curve? (y/n) y
```

```
Interpolate: X =? .2
             Y =   2.40800

Interpolate more points on same curve? (y/n) n

Would you like another run? (y/n) y

Number of Known Points? 11
X of Point 1 ? -5
Y of Point 1 ? .958
X of Point 2 ? -4
Y of Point 2 ? .757
X of Point 3 ? -3
Y of Point 3 ? -.141
X of Point 4 ? -2
Y of Point 4 ? -.909
X of Point 5 ? -1
Y of Point 5 ? -.841
X of Point 6 ? 0
Y of Point 6 ? 0
X of Point 7 ? 1
Y of Point 7 ? .841
X of Point 8 ? 2
Y of Point 8 ? .909
X of Point 9 ? 3
Y of Point 9 ? .141
X of Point 10 ? 4
Y of Point 10 ? -.757
X of Point 11 ? 5
Y of Point 11 ? -.959



Interpolate: X =? -2.47
             Y = -0.62184

Interpolate more points on same curve? (y/n) y

Interpolate: X =? 1.5
             Y =   0.99716

Interpolate more points on same curve? (y/n) n

Would you like another run? (y/n) n
```

Program Listing:

```pascal
program Interpolate(input,output);

const
 maxpoints=50;

type
 index=1..maxpoints;
 arraycord=array[index] of real;

var
 XCord,YCord:arraycord;
 Amount:integer;
 answer:char;
```

84

```
{$I ReadInt}
{$I NotAgain}


procedure ReadData;
var
 i:index;
 X,Y:real;

begin
repeat
  write('Number of Known Points? ');
until ReadInt(Amount,1,maxpoints);
for i:= 1 to Amount do begin
   write('X of Point ',i,' ? ');
   readln(X);
   XCord[i]:=X;
   write('Y of Point ',i,' ? ');
   readln(Y);
   YCord[i]:=Y
   end;   {for i ect.}
writeln;writeln
end;    {procedure ReadData}


procedure Calculate;
var
 Alpha,Beta,IntPol:real;
 i,j:index;

begin
write('Interpolate: X =? ');
readln(IntPol);
Beta:=0;
for i:= 1 to Amount do begin
   Alpha:=1;
   for j:= 1 to Amount do
     if i <> j then
       Alpha:=Alpha*(IntPol-XCord[j])/(XCord[i]-XCord[j]);
   Beta:=Beta + (Alpha * YCord[i])
   end;  {for i to Amount}
writeln('                  Y = ',Beta:1:5);
writeln
end;    {procedure Calculate}
begin   {MAIN}
writeln('Curvilinear Interpolation');
writeln;
repeat
  writeln;
  ReadData;
  repeat
    writeln;
    Calculate;
    write('Interpolate more points on same curve? (y/n) ');
    readln(answer);
    until answer in ['N','n'];
  writeln;
  until NotAgain;
end.   {MAIN}
```

35
Integration: Simpson's Rule

This program approximates the definite integral of a function. The integral is computed using Simpson's rule.

The method the program takes is optional: you must supply either the function of the curve or values of the function at specified intervals. For both methods, you must enter the limits of integration and the increment between points within the limits.

Program Notes

Look at the Pascal function FUNC in the program listing. The function $f(x) = x^3$ becomes the statement

$$\text{FUNC} := \text{INDATA} * \text{INDATA} * \text{INDATA}$$

If you do not wish to integrate the function $f(x) = x^3$, you must change this statement to whatever function you wish to evaluate. The function $f(x) = x^{-2}$ would be expressed

$$\text{FUNC} := 1 / (\text{INDATA} * \text{INDATA})$$

and so on. You need not change any other lines in the program.

If you do not know the equation of the function and will be supplying only values, it does not matter what Pascal statements the function FUNC includes.

Examples:

Find the definite integral of the function $f(x) = x^3$ between 0 and 2 with increments of 0.2 and 0.1.

What is the integral of a curve between -1 and 1 if the points known are as follows:

$(-1,0.54)$	$(0.25,0.969)$
$(-0.75,0.73)$	$(0.5,0.878)$
$(-0.5,0.878)$	$(0.75,0.73)$
$(-0.25,0.969)$	$(1,0.54)$
$(0,1)$	

Run:

```
Integration: Simpson's rule

Do you know the formula? y
Lower limit of integration? 0
Upper limit of integration? 2
Increment of X? .2
Integral is  4.00000
```

```
Integration: Simpson's rule

Do you know the formula? y
Lower limit of integration? 0
Upper limit of integration? 2
Increment of X? .1
Integral is  4.00000
```

```
Integration: Simpson's rule

Do you know the formula? n
Lower limit of integration? -1
Upper limit of integration? 1
Increment of X? .25
Enter first value of F(x)? .54
Enter last value of F(x)? .54
Value of F(x) at interval    1 (X= -0.750 )? .73
Value of F(x) at interval    2 (X= -0.500 )? .878
Value of F(x) at interval    3 (X= -0.250 )? .969
Value of F(x) at interval    4 (X=  0.000 )? 1
Value of F(x) at interval    5 (X=  0.250 )? .969
Value of F(x) at interval    6 (X=  0.500 )? .878
Value of F(x) at interval    7 (X=  0.750 )? .73
Integral is   1.68200
```

Program Listing:

```pascal
program SimpsonsIntegration(input,output);
var  Count : integer;
     LowerLimit, UpperLimit, Result, Step : real;
     StartIntegration, StopIntegration : real;
     Even, Odd : real;
     SubInterval : real;
     KnownFormula : boolean;

{$I ReadReal }
{$I YesNotNo }

function Func(indata : real) : real;
begin
  { Insert your own function here }
  Func := indata * indata * indata
end;

begin
  writeln('Integration: Simpson''s rule');
  writeln;
  write('Do you know the formula? ');
  KnownFormula := YesNotNo;
  repeat
    repeat
      write('Lower limit of integration? ')
    until ReadReal(LowerLimit);
    repeat
      write('Upper limit of integration? ')
    until ReadReal(UpperLimit)
  until LowerLimit < UpperLimit;
  repeat
    repeat
      write('Increment of X? ')
    until ReadReal(Step);
    SubInterval := (UpperLimit - LowerLimit) / Step;
  until SubInterval = trunc(SubInterval);
  if KnownFormula then
    begin
      StartIntegration := func(LowerLimit);
      StopIntegration := func(UpperLimit)
    end
```

```
      else
        begin
          repeat
            write('Enter first value of F(x)? ')
          until ReadReal(StartIntegration);
          repeat
            write('Enter last value of F(x)? ')
          until ReadReal(StopIntegration)
        end;
    Even := 0;
    Odd := 0;
    Count := 1;
    while Count < SubInterval do
      begin
        if KnownFormula then
          Result := Func(LowerLimit + Count * Step)
        else
          repeat
            write('Value of F(x) at interval ', Count:3,
                  ' (X= ', LowerLimit + Count * Step:2:3,' )? ')
          until ReadReal(Result);
        if Count mod 2 = 0 then
          Even := Even + Result
        else
          Odd := Odd + Result;
        Count:=Count + 1
      end;
    writeln('Integral is ', Step/3*(StartIntegration+4*Odd+2*Even+
                                        StopIntegration))
end.
```

36
Integration: Trapezoidal Rule

This program approximates the definite integral of a function using the trapezoidal rule. You must provide the limits of integration, the number of intervals within the limits, and the function to be integrated.

Program Notes

Look at the Pascal function FUNC in the program listing. The function $f(x) = x^3$ becomes the statement
$$FUNC := INDATA * INDATA * INDATA$$

If you do not wish to integrate the function $f(x) = x^3$, you must change this statement to whatever function you wish to evaluate. The function $f(x) = x^{-2}$ would be expressed
$$FUNC := 1 / (INDATA * INDATA)$$

and so on. You need not change any other lines in the program.

Example:

Find the definite integral of the function $f(x) = x^3$ between 0 and 2 with 10 intervals.
    Recalculate the definite integral with 20 intervals.

Run:

```
Integration: Trapezoidal Rule

Enter equal limits to end program
Lower Integration Limit 0
Upper Integration Limit 2
Number of intervals 10
Integral =   4.04000

Lower Integration Limit 0
Upper Integration Limit 2
Number of intervals 20
Integral =   4.01000

Lower Integration Limit 0
Upper Integration Limit 0
```

Program Listing:

```
program Integration(input, output);
var
  LowerLimit, UpperLimit : real;
  NumOfIntervals : integer;
  Result : real;
  Count  : real;
  Step : real;
```

```
{$I ReadReal}
{$I ReadInt}

function GetLimit : boolean;
begin
  repeat
    repeat
      write('Lower Integration Limit ')
    Until ReadReal(LowerLimit);
    repeat
      write('Upper Integration Limit ')
    until ReadReal(UpperLimit);
  until LowerLimit <= UpperLimit;
  GetLimit := LowerLimit <> UpperLimit
end;   { GetLimit }

function Func(InData : real) : real;
begin
  { Insert your own function here }
  Func := InData * InData * InData
end;   { Func }


begin { main }
  writeln('Integration: Trapezoidal Rule');
  writeln;
  writeln('Enter equal limits to end program');
  while GetLimit do
    begin
      repeat
        write('Number of intervals ')
      until ReadInt(NumOfIntervals,1,MaxInt);
      Result := 0;
      Step := (UpperLimit - LowerLimit) / NumOfIntervals;
      Count := LowerLimit;
      while Count <= UpperLimit do
        begin
          Result := Result + Func (Count);
          Count := Count + Step
        end;
      Result := (Result - (Func(LowerLimit) - Func(UpperLimit))/2)* Step;
      writeln('Integral = ', Result);
      writeln
    end
end.
```

37
Integration: Gaussian Quadrature

This program approximates the definite integral of a function. You must provide the limits of integration and the number of intervals within the limits.

The interval of integration is divided into equal subintervals. The definite integral is computed over each subinterval using Gauss's formula. The integrals of the subintervals are summed to give the definite integral of the full interval.

Program Notes

You define the function to be integrated by assigning the Pascal function "FofX" a value. The function is currently $f(x) = x^3$, expressed in Pascal as "FofX := sqr(n) * n". "FofX" must be expressed as a function of the variable "n".

Examples:

Find the definite integral of the function $f(x) = x^3$ between 0 and 2 with 10 and 20 subintervals.

Find the definite integral of the function $f(x) = x^{-2}$ between 1 and 2 and 3 using 10 subintervals.

Run:

```
Gaussian Quadrature

Integration Limits
Lower: 0
Upper: 2
Number of Intervals? 10
Integral = 4.00000

Change Data and Recompute? (y/n) y
Number of Intervals? 20
Integral = 4.00000

Change Data and Recompute? (y/n) n

Would you like another run? (y/n) n
```

Program Listing:

```
program GaussQuad(input,output);
uses transcend; {omit if not Appple Pascal}

const
 maxinput=10;

type
 DataArray=array[1..maxinput] of real;

var
 DataA,DataB:DataArray;

{$I NotAgain}
```

```
function FofX(n:real):real;

begin
 FofX:=sqr(n) * n
end;   {function FofX}


procedure InputData;

begin
DataA[1]:=7.6526521E-2;DataB[1]:=15.275339E-2;
DataA[2]:=22.778585E-2;DataB[2]:=14.917299E-2;
DataA[3]:=37.370609E-2;DataB[3]:=14.209611E-2;
DataA[4]:=51.0867E-2;DataB[4]:=13.168864E-2;
DataA[5]:=63.605386E-2;DataB[5]:=11.819453E-2;
DataA[6]:=74.633191E-2;DataB[6]:=10.193012E-2;
DataA[7]:=83.911697E-2;DataB[7]:=8.3276742E-2;
DataA[8]:=91.223443E-2;DataB[8]:=6.2672048E-2;
DataA[9]:=96.397193E-2;DataB[9]:=4.060143E-2;
DataA[10]:=99.31286E-2;DataB[10]:=1.7614007E-2
end;   {procedure InputData}


procedure Compute;
var
  Sum,Count,Start,AveInt:real;
  Upper,Lower,NumInv:integer;
  Temp:real;
  i,j:integer;
  Answer:char;

begin
writeln;writeln('Integration Limits ');
write('Lower: ');
readln(Lower);
write('Upper: ');
readln(Upper);
Answer:='y';
while Answer in ['y','Y'] do begin
   write('Number of Intervals? ');
   readln(NumInv);
   AveInt:=((Upper - Lower)/NumInv)/2;
   Start:=AveInt + Lower;
   Sum:=0;
   for i:= 1 to NumInv do begin
      Count:=0;
      for j:=1 to maxinput do begin
         Temp:=FofX((AveInt*DataA[j]) + Start) +
               FofX(Start-(AveInt*DataA[j]));
         Count:=(Temp * DataB[j]) + Count
         end;  {for j}
      Sum:=Sum + (Count * AveInt);
      Start:=Start + (2 * AveInt)
      end;  {for i}
   writeln('Integral =',Sum:2:6);
   writeln;write('Change Data and Recompute? (y/n) ');
   readln(Answer)
   end  { while loop}
end;   {procedure Compute}
```

```
begin   {MAIN}
InputData;
writeln;writeln('Gaussian Quadrature');
writeln;
repeat
    writeln;
    Compute;
    writeln;
until NotAgain;
end.    {MAIN}
```

38
Derivative

This program calculates the derivative of a given function at a given point.

Program Notes

The program is currently set up to find the derivative of the function $f(x) = x^2 + cos(x)$, which is defined in the Pascal function FofX. For the statement "FofX := sqr(PointX) + cos(PointX)", substitute any other statement where a function of variable "PointX" is assigned to "FofX".

Example:

Calculate the derivative of the equation $x^2 + cos(x) = 0$ when $x = -1$, $x = 0$, and $x = 1$.

Run:

```
Derivative



Derivative at X= -1
           is -1.15857


Would you like another run? (y/n) y

Derivative at X= 0
           is  0.00000


Would you like another run? (y/n) y

Derivative at X= 1
           is  1.15863


Would you like another run? (y/n) n
```

Program Listing:

```
program Derivative(input,output);
uses transcend;  {omit if not Apple Pascal}


const
 limit=10;

type
 index=1..limit;

var
 PointX:real;
```

DERIVATIVE

```
{$I NotAgain}


function FofX(PointX:real):real;

begin
    FofX:=sqr(PointX) + cos(PointX)
end;

function Inc(Exp:integer):real;
const
 Alpha=5.0E-1;
var
 j:index;
 temp:real;

begin
Temp:=1;
for j:= 1 to Exp do
    Temp:=Temp * Alpha;
Inc:=Temp
end;


procedure Calculate;
var
 Delta,SubDelta,Value:real;
 i:index;

begin
Delta:=0;
for i:= 1 to limit do begin
    SubDelta:=Delta;
    Value:=PointX + Inc(i);
    Delta:=(FofX(Value) - FofX(PointX))/(Value-PointX)
    end;
writeln('                    is ',((2*Delta)-SubDelta):3:6);
writeln
end;


begin {MAIN}
writeln;
writeln('Derivative');
writeln;writeln;
 repeat
    writeln;
    write('Derivative at X= ');
    readln(PointX);
    Calculate;
    writeln;
until NotAgain
end. {MAIN}
```

39
Roots of Quadratic Equations

This program calculates the roots of a quadratic equation in the form

$$ax^2 + bx + c = 0$$

where a, b, and c are real coefficients.

The formula used to calculate the roots is

$$\text{root} = \frac{-b \pm \sqrt{b^2 - 4 \cdot a \cdot c}}{2 \cdot a}$$

Examples:

What are the roots of the equation $2x^2 + x - 1 = 0$?
    Calculate the roots of the quadratic equation $x^2 + 4x + 6 = 0$.

Run:

```
Roots of Quadratic Equations

Coefficient A: 2
Coefficient B: 1
Coefficient C: -1
Real roots: -1.00000   0.500000

Would you like another run? (y/n) y

Coefficient A: 1
Coefficient B: 4
Coefficient C: 6
Complex roots: -2.00000   + or -   1.41421   i

Would you like another run? (y/n) n
```

Program Listing:

```
program quadratic(input, output);
uses transcendentals; { omit this line if not using Apple Pascal }
var
   a, b, c, d { discriminant }, r: real;

{$I ReadReal}
{$I NotAgain}
```

```
begin { main }
  writeln('Roots of Quadratic Equations');
  repeat
    writeln;
    repeat
      write('Coefficient a: ')
    until ReadReal(a);
    repeat
      write('Coefficient b: ')
    until ReadReal(b);
    repeat
      write('Coefficient c: ')
    until ReadReal(c);
    d := sqr(b) - 4 * a * c; { discriminant }
    r := sqrt(abs(d));
    if d >= 0 then
      writeln('Real roots: ',(-b - r) / (2 * a):12:6, (-b + r)
                                          / (2 * a):12:6)
    else
      writeln('Complex roots: ', -b / (2 * a):12:6,
              ' + OR - ', r / (2 * a):12:6, ' i');
    writeln
  until NotAgain
end.
```

40
Real Roots of Polynomials: Newton

This program calculates real roots of a polynomial with real coefficients. You must give an estimate of each root.

The calculations are performed using Newton's method for approximating roots of equations. The value of the error and derivative are included for each root calculated.

Program Notes

The constant "MaxDegree" must be set equal to the maximum degree of the equation.

Example:

Find the roots of $4x^4 - 2.5x^2 - x + 0.5$

Run:

```
Real Roots of Polynomials: Newton

Degree of equation: 4
Coefficient entry:
  Constant: .5
  Coefficient of degree 1: -1
  Coefficient of degree 2: -2.5
  Coefficient of degree 3: 0
  Coefficient of degree 4: 4

guess: -.8

Root            Error           Derivative
 3.03576E-1   -2.98023E-8       -2.07025

Menu:
    Find root of existing function
    Enter new function & find root
    Quit

F,E,Q: q
```

Program Listing:

```
program RealRootsNewton(input,output);
const  MaxDegree= 10;

type   Coefficients = array[0..MaxDegree] of real;

var    Polynomial, Derivative : Coefficients;
       degree : integer;
       ch : char;
       quit : boolean;
```

```
{$I ReadReal}
{$I ReadInt}


procedure GetInput;
var  h : integer;

begin
  for h:=0 to MaxDegree do
    begin
      Polynomial[h]:= 0;
      Derivative[h]:= 0
    end;
  repeat
    write('Degree of equation: ')
  until ReadInt(degree, 1, MaxDegree);
  writeln('Coefficient entry:');
  for h:=0 to degree do
    if h=0 then
      repeat
        write('  Constant: ')
      until ReadReal(Polynomial[h])
    else
      repeat
        write('  Coefficient of degree ',h,': ')
      until ReadReal(Polynomial[h]);
  for h:=0 to degree-1  do
    Derivative[h]:= Polynomial[h+1] * (h+1)
end;  { procedure GetInput }


procedure CalculateRoots;
var  h, count : integer;
     X, guess, NextGuess, ValueOfDerivative, ValueOfPolynomial : real;
     answer : char;
     GuessAgain, continue, found : boolean;


begin
  found:= false;
  GuessAgain:= true;
  continue:= true;
  repeat
    ValueOfPolynomial:= 0;
    ValueOfDerivative:= 0;
    if GuessAgain then
      repeat
        write('guess: ');
        count:= 0;
        GuessAgain:= false
      until ReadReal(guess);
    count:=count+1;
    X:= 1;
    for h:=0 to degree do
      begin
        ValueOfPolynomial:= ValueOfPolynomial + Polynomial[h] * X;
        ValueOfDerivative:= ValueOfDerivative + Derivative[h] * X;
        X:= X * guess
      end;
```

```
      if ValueOfDerivative = 0 then
        begin
          writeln('Derivative=0 at x= ',guess);
          write('  Continue? (y/n) ');
          readln(answer);
          continue:= answer in ['y','Y'];
          GuessAgain:= true
        end
      else
        begin
          NextGuess:= guess - ValueOfPolynomial / ValueOfDerivative;
          if NextGuess=guess then
            found:= true
          else
            begin
              guess:= NextGuess;
              if count>100 then
                begin
                  writeln('100 iterations completed');
                  writeln('   x= ',guess,' F(x)= ',ValueOfPolynomial);
                  write('Do you want to continue? (y/n) ');
                  readln(answer);
                  continue:= answer in ['y','Y'];
                  count:= 0
                end
            end { if NextGuess=guess }
        end { else (ValueOfDerivative<>0) }
    until found or not continue ;
    if guess=NextGuess then
      begin
        writeln;
        writeln('Root              Error         Derivative');
        writeln(guess,ValueOfPolynomial:13,ValueOfDerivative:14)
      end
end;  { procedure CalculateRoots }


begin  { main }
  writeln;writeln('Real Roots of Polynomials: Newton');
  writeln;
  quit:= false;
  GetInput;
  writeln;
  CalculateRoots;
  repeat
    writeln;
    writeln('Menu:');
    writeln('   Find root of existing function');
    writeln('   Enter new function & find root');
    writeln('   Quit');
    writeln;
    repeat
      write('F,E,Q: ');
      readln(ch)
    until ch in ['f','e','q','F','E','Q'];
    writeln;
    case ch of
      'f','F' : CalculateRoots;
      'e','E' : begin
                  GetInput;
                  writeln;
```

```
                    end;
        'q','Q' : quit:= true
      end
   until quit= true
end.
```

41
Roots of Polynomials: Half-Interval Search

This program calculates roots of polynomials within a given interval. The program first conducts a random search within the given interval for two points with opposite signs. If a change of sign is found, then the root is calculated by the half-interval search method. If no change of sign is found, you will enter another interval.

Program Notes

You must enter the function whose roots will be found, and the program will guide you through the entry, asking for degree and coefficient of each term.

Be aware of the following as you run the program:

1. There may be a delay of up to one minute while the program is searching for roots when particularly complex calculations must be performed.
2. If the difference between the roots is very small, the opposite signs may not be found. If the difference is beyond the discriminatory ability of your computer, the program will necessarily fail to find the difference.
3. If the low point is very close to zero, a nonexistent root may be calculated because of round-off.
4. If the function has degree larger than 6, the program may have difficulty calculating roots. To minimize this problem, avoid entering an interval which includes 0, unless 0 is one of the endpoints.

Example:

Find a root of the function $f(x) = 4x^4 - 2.5x^2 - x + .5$.

Run:

```
Roots of Polynomials : Half-Interval Search

Function Entry
  Number of terms: 4
  Term 1      Coefficient: .5
              Exponent: 0
  Term 2      Coefficient: -1
              Exponent: 1
  Term 3      Coefficient: -2.5
              Exponent: 2
  Term 4      Coefficient: 4
              Exponent: 4

Menu:
  Enter new function
  Find roots of existing function
  Quit

E,F,Q: f
```

```
Interval
  Lower limit: -1
  UpperLimit: 0

Searching for change of sign...

No change of sign found

Menu:
  Enter new function
  Find roots of existing function
  Quit

E,F,Q: f
Interval
  Lower limit: 0
  UpperLimit: 1

Searching for change of sign...

Root =  3.03576E-1

Menu:
  Enter new function
  Find roots of existing function
  Quit

E,F,Q: q
```

Program Listing:

```
program RootsHalfInterval(input,output);
uses transcend;  { Omit if not using Apple Pascal }
type   TermPointer = ^term;
       term = record
                 coefficient : real;
                 exponent : integer;
                 next : TermPointer
              end;
       SignType = -1..1;

var  FirstTerm, LastTerm, heap : TermPointer;
     LowerLimit, UpperLimit : real;
     NumTerms : integer;
     quit : boolean;
     ch : char;

{$I ReadInt }
{$I ReadReal }
{$I IntRaise }


procedure Initialize;
begin
  FirstTerm:= nil;
  LastTerm:= nil;
  heap:= nil;
  quit:= false;
end;  { procedure Initialize }
```

```pascal
procedure GetTerm;
var  p : TermPointer;
begin
  if heap = nil then
    new(p)
  else
    begin
      p:= heap;
      heap:= heap^.next
    end;
  if FirstTerm = nil then
    FirstTerm:= p
  else  LastTerm^.next:= p;
  LastTerm:= p;
  LastTerm^.next:= nil
end;  { procedure GetTerm }


procedure DisposeOfPolynomial;
var  p : TermPointer;
begin
  if heap <> nil then
    LastTerm^.next:= heap;
  heap:= FirstTerm;
  FirstTerm:= nil;
  LastTerm:= nil
end;  { DisposeOfPolynomial }


function SignOfFn(x : real) : SignType;
var  p : TermPointer;
     value : real;

begin
  value:= 0;
  p:= FirstTerm;
  while p<>nil do
    begin
      value:= value + p^.coefficient * IntRaise(x,p^.exponent);
      p:=p^.next
    end;
  if value > 0 then
    SignOfFn:= 1
  else
    if value < 0 then
      SignOfFn:= -1
    else SignOfFn:= 0
end;  { function SignOfFn }


procedure GetInput;
begin
  writeln('Interval');
  repeat
    write('  Lower limit: ')
  until ReadReal(LowerLimit);
  repeat
    write('  UpperLimit: ')
  until ReadReal(UpperLimit) and (UpperLimit > LowerLimit);
end;  { procedure GetInput }
```

```
procedure EnterFunction;
var  h : integer;

begin
  writeln('Function Entry');
  repeat
    write('  Number of terms: ')
  until  ReadInt(NumTerms, 1, maxint);
  for h:=1 to NumTerms do
    begin
      GetTerm;
      write('  Term ',h);
      with LastTerm^ do
        begin
          repeat
            write('    Coefficient: ')
          until ReadReal(coefficient) and (coefficient<>0);
          repeat
            write('Exponent: ':25)
          until ReadInt(exponent, 0, 35)
        end
    end  { for h }
end;  { procedure EnterFunction }


function ChangeOfSign : SignType;
var  level : integer;
     FirstSign, SecondSign : SignType;
     ChangeFound : boolean;

  function half(low,high : real) : boolean;
  var mid : real;
      MidSign : SignType;

  begin
    level:= level + 1;
    if level = 11 then
      half:= false
    else
      begin
        mid:= (low + high) / 2;
        MidSign:= SignOfFn(mid);
        if FirstSign * MidSign = 1 then
          if half(mid,high) then
            half:= true
          else
            if half(low,mid) then
              half:= true
            else  half:= false
        else
          begin
            half:= true;
            UpperLimit:= mid
          end
      end;
    level:= level - 1
  end; {function half (inside function ChangeOfSign) }

  begin
    writeln;writeln('Searching for change of sign...');
    writeln;
    level:= 0;
```

```
    FirstSign:= SignOfFn(LowerLimit);
    SecondSign:= SignOfFn(UpperLimit);
    if FirstSign * SecondSign = 1 then
      ChangeFound:= half(LowerLimit,UpperLimit);
    ChangeOfSign:= FirstSign * SignOfFn(UpperLimit)
  end;  { function ChangeofSign }


procedure FindRoot;
var  NegativeLimit, PositiveLimit, MidPoint, NextMidPoint : real;
     SignOfMidPoint : SignType;

begin
  if SignOfFn(LowerLimit) = -1 then
    begin
      NegativeLimit:= LowerLimit;
      PositiveLimit:= UpperLimit
    end
  else
    begin
      NegativeLimit:= UpperLimit;
      PositiveLimit:= LowerLimit
    end;
  NextMidPoint:= (NegativeLimit + PositiveLimit) / 2;
  repeat
    MidPoint:= NextMidPoint;
    SignOfMidPoint:= SignOfFn(MidPoint);
    if SignOfMidPoint = -1 then
      NegativeLimit:= MidPoint
    else PositivePoint:= MidPoint;
    NextMidPoint:= (NegativeLimit + PositiveLimit) / 2;
  until (MidPoint=NextMidPoint) or (abs(MidPoint)<1E-5);
  if abs(MidPoint) < 1E-5 then
    begin
      write('Root is too close to zero to calculate. ');
      writeln('best estimate of');
    end;
  writeln('Root = ',MidPoint)
end;  { procedure FindRoot }


begin  { main }
  writeln;writeln('Roots of Polynomials : Half-Interval Search');
  writeln;
  Initialize;
  EnterFunction;
  repeat
    writeln;
    writeln('Menu: ');
    writeln('  Enter new function');
    writeln('  Find roots of existing function');
    writeln('  Quit');
    writeln;
    repeat
      write('E,F,Q: ');
      readln(ch);
    until ch in ['E','F','Q','e','f','q'];
    case ch of
      'e','E' : EnterFunction;
      'f','F' : begin
                  GetInput;
```

```
                case ChangeOfSign of
                  1 : writeln('No change of sign found');
                 -1 : FindRoot;
                  0 : if SignOfFn(UpperLimit) = 0 then
                        writeln('Root = ',UpperLimit)
                      else writeln('Root = ',LowerLimit)
                end   { case ChangeOfSign }
              end;
      'q','Q' : quit:= true
    end   { case ch of }
  until quit
end.
```

42
Trig Polynomial

This program solves a trigonometric function for a given angle. The function must be in the following form:

$$f(x) = A_1 \sin(x) + B_1 \cos(x) + A_2 \sin(2x) + B_2 \sin(2x) ... + A_n \sin(n \cdot x) + B_n \cos(n \cdot x)$$

where n = the number of pairs of coefficients.

You will be prompted to enter the coefficients.

Example:

Solve the following equation when the angle equals 45°, 90°, and 105°:

$$f(x) = \sin(x) + 2 \cdot \cos(x) - 2 \cdot \sin(2x) + \cos(2x) + 5 \cdot \sin(3x) - 3 \cdot \cos(3x)$$

Run:

```
Trigonometric Polynomial

Coefficient Entry:

Number of coefficient pairs: 3
Pair 1:
  Sin(1x) coefficient: 1
  Cos(1x) coefficient: 2
Pair 2:
  Sin(2x) coefficient: -2
  Cos(2x) coefficient: 1
Pair 3:
  Sin(3x) coefficient: 5
  Cos(3x) coefficient: -3

Menu:
  New coefficients
  Calculation
  Quit

N, C, Q ? c
Enter angle in degrees.
Enter -1 to return to menu

Angle: 45
F( 4.50000E1) =  5.77818

Angle: 90
F( 9.00000E1) = -5.00000

Angle: 105
F( 1.05000E2) = -5.07459

Angle: -1
```

```
Menu:
  New coefficients
  Calculation
  Quit

N, C, Q ? q
```

Program Listing:

```pascal
program TrigRoots(input,output);
uses transcend;  { Omit if not using Apple Pascal }

type CPairPointer = ^CoefficientPair;
     CoefficientPair = record
                         SinCoefficient,
                         CosCoefficient : real;
                         next : CPairPointer
                       end;

var  FirstCoefficient, LastCoefficient, heap : CPairPointer;
     angle, AngleInRadians : real;
     NumPairs : integer;
     quit : boolean;
     ch : char;
     CorrectInput : set of char;

{$I ReadInt }
{$I ReadReal }


procedure Initialize;
begin
  heap:= nil;
  FirstCoefficient:= nil;
  LastCoefficient:= nil;
  quit:= false;
  NumPairs:= 0;
  angle:= 0;
  CorrectInput:= ['n','N','c','C','q','Q']
end;  { procedure Initialize }


function radians(angle : real) : real;
const  pi = 3.141592654;
begin
  radians:= angle * pi / 180
end;  { function radians }


procedure GetCoefficientPair;
var  p : CPairPointer;

begin
  if heap = nil then new(p)
  else
    begin
      p:= heap;
      heap:= heap^.next
    end;
  if FirstCoefficient = nil then
    FirstCoefficient:= p
```

```
    else
      LastCoefficient^.next:= p;
    LastCoefficient:= p;
    LastCoefficient^.next:= nil
end;   { procedure GetCoefficientPair }


procedure DisposeOfCoefficients;
begin
    if heap <> nil then
      LastCoefficient^.next:= heap;
    heap:= FirstCoefficient;
    FirstCoefficient:= nil;
    LastCoefficient:= nil
end;   { procedure DisposeOfCoefficients }


procedure GetNewCoefficients;
var  h : integer;

begin
    writeln('Coefficient Entry:');
    writeln;
    repeat
      write('Number of coefficient pairs: ')
    until ReadInt(NumPairs, 1, maxint);
    for h:=1 to NumPairs do
      begin
        GetCoefficientPair;
        writeln('Pair ',h,':');
        repeat
          write('  Sin(',h,'x) coefficient: ')
        until ReadReal(LastCoefficient^.SinCoefficient);
        repeat
          write('  Cos(',h,'x) coefficient: ')
        until ReadReal(LastCoefficient^.CosCoefficient);
      end
end;   { procedure GetNewCoefficients }


procedure Calculate;
var  h : integer;
     sum, A, B : real;
     CurrentCoefficient : CPairPointer;

begin
  writeln;
  repeat
    write('Angle: ')
  until ReadReal(angle);
  if angle>=0 then
    begin
      CurrentCoefficient:= FirstCoefficient;
      sum:= 0;
      AngleInRadians:= radians(angle);
      for h:=1 to NumPairs do
        begin
          A:= CurrentCoefficient^.SinCoefficient;
          B:= CurrentCoefficient^.CosCoefficient;
          sum:= sum + A * sin(h * AngleInRadians) +
                                B * cos(h * AngleInRadians);
```

```
            CurrentCoefficient:= CurrentCoefficient^.next
         end;
      if abs(sum) < 1E-6 then sum:= 0;
      writeln('F(',angle,') = ',sum)
   end
end;  { procedure Calculate }


begin  { main }
  writeln; writeln('Trigonometric Polynomial');
  writeln;
  Initialize;
  GetNewCoefficients;
  writeln;
  repeat
    writeln('Menu:');
    writeln('  New coefficients');
    writeln('  Calculation');
    writeln('  Quit');
    writeln;
    repeat
      write('N, C, Q ? ');
      readln(ch)
    until ch in CorrectInput;
    case ch of
      'n','N' : begin
                   DisposeOfCoefficients;
                   GetNewCoefficients
                end;

      'c','C' : begin
                   writeln('Enter angle in degrees.');
                   writeln('Enter -1 to return to menu');
                   while angle >= 0 do
                      Calculation;
                   angle:=0
                end;

      'q','Q' : quit:= true
    end;
    writeln
  until quit
end.
```

43
Simultaneous Equations

This program solves a system of linear equations. The number of unknown coefficients in each equation must equal the number of equations being solved. You must enter the coefficients of each equation.

Program Notes

This program allows no more than 10 simultaneous equations. The maximum is set with the constant "MaxEquations." Note that if you change MaxEquations, you must also change the constant "PlusMax," which equals one (1) more than the constant MaxEquations.

Example:

Solve the following system of equations:

$$x_1 + 2x_2 + 3x_3 = 4$$
$$3x_1 + 6x_2 = 1$$
$$-3x_1 + 4x_2 - 2x_3 = 0$$

Run:

```
Simultaneous Equations


Number of Equations: 3
Coefficient Matrix
Equation 1
  Coefficient 1: 1
  Coefficient 2: 2
  Coefficient 3: 3
  Constant: 4
Equation 2
  Coefficient 1: 3
  Coefficient 2: 6
  Coefficient 3: 0
  Constant: 1
Equation 3
  Coefficient 1: -3
  Coefficient 2: 4
  Coefficient 3: -2
  Constant: 0
x 1 =-0.355556
x 2 = 0.344445
x 3 = 1.22222

Would you like another run? (y/n) n
```

Program Listing:

```
program SimulEquations (input,output);

const
 MaxEquations=10;
 PlusMax=11;

type
 index=1..Maxequations;
 MatrixArray =array [index,1..PlusMax] of real;

var
 Matrix:MatrixArray;
 NumEquations:index;
 NoSolution:boolean;

{$I ReadInt}
{$I NotAgain}


procedure ReadData;
var
 i,j:integer;
 Coeff:real;

begin
writeln;
repeat
   write('Number of Equations: ');
until ReadInt (NumEquations,1,MaxEquations);
writeln('Coefficient Matrix');
for i:= 1 to NumEquations do begin
   writeln('Equation ',i);
   for j:= 1 to NumEquations do begin
       write('  Coefficient ',j,': ');
       readln(Coeff);
       Matrix[i,j]:=Coeff
       end;  {if j}
   write('  Constant: ');
   readln(Coeff);
   Matrix[i,j]:=Coeff
end  {for i}
end;  {procedure ReadData}


procedure Swap(i,j:index);
var
 count:integer;
 Temp:real;

begin
for count:= 1 to (NumEquations + 1) do begin
     Temp:=Matrix[i,count];
     Matrix[i,count]:=Matrix[j,count];
     Matrix[j,count]:=Temp
     end  {for count}
end; {procedure Swap}
```

```
procedure Subtract(computed:index);
var
 i,k,count:integer;
 Temp:real;

begin
Temp:=1/Matrix[computed,computed];
for count:=1 to (NumEquations + 1) do
    Matrix[computed,count]:=Temp*Matrix[computed,count];
for i:=1 to NumEquations do
     if i <> computed then begin
          Temp:=(-Matrix[i,computed]);
          for k:= 1 to (NumEquations + 1) do
               Matrix[i,k]:=Matrix[i,k] + (Temp * Matrix[computed,k]);
          end  {if i <> Computed}
end;  {procedure Subtract}


procedure Calculate;
var
 computed,count:index;

begin
NoSolution:=false;  {initialize for entering loop}
computed:=1;
while (computed <= NumEquations) and (not NoSolution) do begin
     NoSolution:=true;  {reset for test}
     count:=computed;
     while (count<=NumEquations) and (NoSolution) do
         if Matrix[count,computed] <> 0 then
           NoSolution:=false
         else
           count:=count + 1;
     if not NoSolution then begin
         Swap(computed,count);
         Subtract(computed)
         end;  {if not NoSolution}
     computed:=computed + 1
     end  {while loop}
end;  {procedure Calculate}


procedure Print;
var
 i,j:integer;

begin
for i:=1 to NumEquations do
    writeln('x ',i,' =',Matrix[i,NumEquations+1]:1:6);
end;  {procedure Print}



begin {Main}
writeln;writeln('Simultaneous Equations');
writeln;
repeat
  ReadData;
  Calculate;
```

```
   if NoSolution then begin
     writeln;writeln('No Unique Solution');
     writeln;
     end    {if NoSolution}
   else
     Print;
writeln;
until NotAgain
end.   {Main}
```

44

Linear Programming

Courtesy: Harold Hange
Earlham College
Richmond, Indiana

This program uses the simplex method to solve a linear programming problem. You will be asked for the number of constraints and the number of variables. You must also enter the coefficient, relation, and constant for each variable.

Program Notes

You may have no more than ten variables or constraints.

Please note that since constants and variables need not conform with English spelling rules, there is a variable named "Varible" and a procedure named "Artifical." Be sure that you spell them as they appear in the listing.

Example:

A manufacturer wishes to produce 100 pounds of an alloy which is 83% lead, 14% iron, and 3% antimony. He has available five alloys with the following compositions and prices:

Alloy 1	Alloy 2	Alloy 3	Alloy 4	Alloy 5
90	80	95	70	30
5	5	2	30	70
5	15	3	0	0
$6.13	$7.12	$5.85	$4.57	$3.96

How should he combine these alloys to get the desired product at minimum cost?
Note that this problem results in the following system of equations:

$$x_1 + x_2 + x_3 + x_4 + x_5 = 100$$
$$0.90x_1 + 0.80x_2 + 0.95x_3 + 0.70x_4 + 0.30x_5 = 83$$
$$0.05x_1 + 0.05x_2 + 0.02x_3 + 0.30x_4 + 0.70x_5 = 14$$
$$0.05x_1 + 0.15x_2 + 0.03x_3 = 3$$
$$6.13x_1 + 7.12x_2 + 5.85x_3 + 4.57x_4 + 3.96x_5 = Z \text{ (min)}$$

Run:

```
Linear Programming

Is the problem a Minimization or Maximization (min/max) : min

How many variables: 5
How many Constraints: 8
```

```
For Constraint 1 what is
Variable 1 : 1
Variable 2 : 1
Variable 3 : 1
Variable 4 : 1
Variable 5 : 1
Quantity of Constraint 1 : 100
The relation for Constraint 1 (< , = , >) : <
For Constraint 2 what is
Variable 1 : 1
Variable 2 : 1
Variable 3 : 1
Variable 4 : 1
Variable 5 : 1
Quantity of Constraint 2 : 1000
The relation for Constraint 2 (< , = , >) : >
For Constraint 3 what is
Variable 1 : .9
Variable 2 : .8
Variable 3 : .95
Variable 4 : .7
Variable 5 : .3
Quantity of Constraint 3 : 83
The relation for Constraint 3 (< , = , >) : <
For Constraint 4 what is
Variable 1 : .9
Variable 2 : .8
Variable 3 : .95
Variable 4 : .7
Variable 5 : .3
Quantity of Constraint 4 : 83
The relation for Constraint 4 (< , = , >) : >
For Constraint 5 what is
Variable 1 : .05
Variable 2 : .05
Variable 3 : .02
Variable 4 : .3
Variable 5 : .7
Quantity of Constraint 5 : 14
The relation for Constraint 5 (< , = , >) : <
For Constraint 6 what is
Variable 1 : .05
Variable 2 : .05
Variable 3 : .02
Variable 4 : .3
Variable 5 : .7
Quantity of Constraint 6 : 14
The relation for Constraint 6 (< , = , >) : >
For Constraint 7 what is
Variable 1 : .05
Variable 2 : .15
Variable 3 : .03
Variable 4 : 0
Variable 5 : 0
Quantity of Constraint 7 : 3
The relation for Constraint 7 (< , = , >) : <
For Constraint 8 what is
Variable 1 : .05
Variable 2 : .15
Variable 3 : .03
Variable 4 : 0
```

```
Variable 5 : 0
Quantity of Constraint 8 : 3
The relation for Constraint 8 (< , = , >) : >

The Profit for Variable 1 : 6.13
The Profit for Variable 2 : 7.12
The Profit for Variable 3 : 5.85
The Profit for Variable 4 : 4.57
The Profit for Variable 5 : 3.96

Answers
Variable 2 =   10.4348
Variable 3 =   47.8261
Variable 4 =   41.7391

Total value of Objective Function is   544.826

Would you like another run? (y/n) n
```

Program Listing:

```pascal
program Linear(input,output);

const
 MaxInput=10;
 MaxTable=30;

type
 Index=1..MaxInput;
 Range=1..MaxTable;
 MatrixArray=array [Index,Range] of real;
 HeaderArray=array [Range] of real;
 RelArray=array[Index] of char;

var
 Matrix:MatrixArray;
 SolMix,Quantity,Ccolumn,Crow,Zrow,CminusZ:HeaderArray;
 Relation:RelArray;
 Constraints,Varibles:Index;
 TotalVaribles:Range;
 OverQuantity,OverPriced:real;
 MinProblem:Boolean;

 {$I ReadInt}
 {$I NotAgain}

procedure CalcZrow;
var
j:Range;
i:Index;
Total:real;

begin
for j:=1 to TotalVarible do begin
     Total:=0;
     for i:= 1 to Constraints do
          Total:=(Ccolumn[i] * Matrix[i,j]) + Total;
     Zrow[j]:=Total
     end   {for j}
end;    {procedure CalZrow}
```

```
procedure CalcCminusZ;
var
  j:Range;

begin
for j:= 1 to TotalVarible do
      CminusZ[j]:=Crow[J]-Zrow[j]
end;    {procedure CalcCminusZ}



procedure Artifical(i:Index; TotalVaribles:Range);

begin
if MinProblem then begin
    Crow[TotalVaribles]:=OverPriced;
    Ccolumn[i]:=OverPriced
    end  {if Minimization}
else begin
    Crow[TotalVarible]:=(-OverPriced);
    Ccolumn[i]:=OverPriced
    end;  {if Maximization}
Matrix[i,TotalVariables]:=1
end;  {procedure Artifical}



  procedure AddSlack;
  var
   j:Range;
   i:Index;

  begin
  TotalVaribles:=Varibles;
  for i:= 1 to Constraints do begin
      TotalVaribles:=TotalVaribles + 1;
      if Relation[i] = '<' then begin
          Matrix[i,TotalVaribles]:=1;
          Ccolumn[i]:=0;
          Crow[TotalVaribles]:=0
          end  {if <}
      else if Relation[i] = '=' then
          Artifical(i,TotalVaribles)
      else begin    {else >}
          Artifical(i,TotalVaribles);
          TotalVaribles:=Totalvaribles + 1;
          Matrix[i,TotalVaribles]:=(-1);
          Crow[TotalVaribles]:=0
          end    {else >}
      end  {for i}
  end;  {procedure AddSlack}

  procedure SetTable;
  var
   OneChar:char;
   i:Index;
   k,j:Range;
   Temp:real;
```

```
begin
for i:=1 to MaxInput do    {Initialize Matrix to zeros}
    for j:=1 to MaxTable do
        Matrix[i,j]:=0;
for i:= 1 to MaxInput do
    SolMix[i]:=0;
OverQuantity:=0;
for i:= 1 to Constraints do begin  {read in the data}
    writeln('For Constraint ',i,' what is');
    for j:= 1 to Varibles do begin
        write('Variable ',j,' : ');
        readln(Temp);
        Matrix[i,j]:=Temp
        end;  {for j}
    write('Quantity of Constraint ',i,' : ');
    readln(Temp);
    Quantity[i]:=Temp;
    OverQuantity:=OverQuantity + Temp;
    OneChar:=' ';
    while not (OneChar in ['<','=','>']) do begin
        write('The relation for Constraint ',i,' (< , = , >) : ');
        readln(OneChar);
        Relation[i]:=OneChar
        end  {while not in OneChar}
    end;  {for i}
writeln;
OverPriced:=0;
for i:= 1 to Varibles do begin
    write('The Profit for Variable ',i,' : ');
    readln(Temp);
    Crow[i]:=Temp;
    OverPriced:=OverPriced + Temp
    end  {for i, to read in prices}
 end;  {procedure SetTable}

 procedure ReadData;
 var
  charstring:string[4];
  complete:boolean;

 begin
 complete:=false;
 while not complete do begin
        write('Is the problem a Minimization or Maximization (min/max) : ');
        readln(charstring);
        if (charstring = 'MIN' ) or (charstring = 'min') then begin
            complete:=true;
            MinProblem:=true
            end  {if charstring in min}
        else if (charstring = 'MAX') or (charstring = 'max') then begin
            complete:=true;
            MinProblem:=true
            end  {else if}
        end;  {while not complete}
writeln;
repeat
  write('How many Variables: ');
until ReadInt (Varibles,1,MaxInput);
repeat
  write('How many Constraints: ');
until ReadInt (Constraints,1,MaxInput);
```

120

```
writeln;
SetTable
end;   {procedure ReadData}


  procedure ReviseRows (BestRow:Index; BestColumn:Range);
  var
   Intersection:real;
   i:Index;
   k:Range;

  begin
  for i:= 1 to Constraints do begin
       if BestRow <> i then begin
             Intersection:=Matrix[i,BestColumn];
             for k:= 1 to TotalVariables do
                 Matrix[i,k]:=Matrix[i,k] - (Intersection * Matrix[BestRow,k]);
             Quantity[i]:=Quantity[i] - (Intersection * Quantity[BestRow])
          end   {if BestRow}
       end   {for Constraints}
end;   {procedure ReviseRows}

procedure FirstRow (BestColumn:Range);
var
 BestRow:Index;
 i:Index;
 k:Range;
 Intersection,Best:real;

begin
Best:=OverQuantity;   {initialize to high number}
for i:= 1 to Constraints do
     if Matrix[i,BestColumn] <> 0 then begin
          if ((Quantity[i] / Matrix[i,BestColumn]) < Best) and
                         ((Quantity[i] / Matrix[i,BestColumn]) > 0) then begin
               Best:=Quantity[i] / Matrix[i,BestColumn];
               BestRow:=i
               end   {if  < Best}
          end;    {if Matrix}
Intersection:=Matrix[BestRow,BestColumn];
for k:= 1 to TotalVaribles do
     Matrix[BestRow,k]:=Matrix[BestRow,k] / Intersection;
Quantity[BestRow]:=Quantity[BestRow] / Intersection;
SolMix[BestRow]:=BestColumn;
Ccolumn[BestRow]:=Crow[BestColumn];
ReviseRows(BestRow,BestColumn)
end;   {procudure Fix}

procedure Calculate;
var
 Best:real;
 k,BestColumn:range;
 efficent:boolean;

begin
efficent:=false;
while not efficent do begin
      Best:=0;
      for k:= 1 to TotalVaribles do
           if MinProblem then begin
               if CminusZ[k] < Best then begin
```

```
                          Best:=CminusZ[k];
                          BestColumn:=k
                       end  {if CminusZ < Best}
                   end  {if Problem}
              else begin
                  if CminusZ[k] > Best then begin
                          Best:=CminusZ[k];
                          BestColumn:=k
                       end  {if CminusZ > Best}
                  end;  {else Maximization}
       if Best <> 0 then
            FirstRow(BestColumn)
       else
            efficent:=true;
       CalcZrow;
       CalcCminusZ;
       end  {while not efficent}
end;  {procedure Calculate}

procedure PrintResults;
var
 i:Index;
 Temp:integer;
 TempOne,Total:real;

begin
Total:=0;
writeln;writeln('Answers');
for i:= 1 to Constraints do begin
     Temp:=trunc(SolMix[i]);
     if (Ccolumn[i] > 0) and (Temp > 0) and (Quantity[i] >0) then begin
          TempOne:=Quantity[i];
          writeln('Variable ',Temp,' = ',TempOne:1:6);
          Total:=Total + (Quantity[i] * Ccolumn[i])
          end  {if Ccolumn}
     end;  {for i}
 writeln;writeln('Total value of Objective Function is ',Total:1:6);
 writeln;
 end;  {procedure PrintResults}

begin  {Main}
writeln;writeln('Linear Programming');writeln;
repeat
  ReadData;
  AddSlack;
  CalcZrow;
  CalcCminusZ;
  Calculate;
  PrintResults;
until NotAgain
end.  {Main}
```

45

Matrix Addition, Subtraction, Scalar Multiplication

This program adds or subtracts two matrices, or multiplies a matrix by a given scalar. You must input the value of each element of each matrix. To perform addition or subtraction the dimensions of the two matrices must be equal.

Program Notes

The program is currently set to accept no more than three rows and three columns in each matrix. You can increase or decrease these limits by altering the constants "MaxRows" and "MaxCols" respectively. Operations with large matrices may tax the memory space of your computer.

Example:

Find the sum of the following matrices, then multiply the resultant matrix by 3.

$$\begin{bmatrix} 1 & 0 & -1 \\ 5 & 8 & 0.5 \\ -1 & 2 & 0 \end{bmatrix} \quad \begin{bmatrix} -5 & -1 & 2 \\ 6 & -0.1 & 0 \\ 3 & 4 & -2 \end{bmatrix}$$

Run:

```
Matrix Addition, Subtraction, and Scalar Multiplication

Operations are:
    Addition
    Subtraction
    Multiplication by a scalar

operation (a, s, m): a

Matrix dimensions:
    Number of Rows: 3
    Number of Cols: 3

Matrix 1:
  Row 1
    Value in column 1: 1
    Value in column 2: 0
    Value in column 3: -1
  Row 2
    Value in column 1: 5
    Value in column 2: 8
    Value in column 3: .5
  Row 3
    Value in column 1: -1
    Value in column 2: 2
    Value in column 3: 0
```

```
Matrix 2:
  Row 1
    Value in column 1: -5
    Value in column 2: -1
    Value in column 3: 2
  Row 2
    Value in column 1: 6
    Value in column 2: -.1
    Value in column 3: 0
  Row 3
    Value in column 1: 3
    Value in column 2: 4
    Value in column 3: -2


    -4.00000       -1.00000        1.00000
  1.10000E1        7.90000    5.00000E-1
    2.00000        6.00000       -2.00000
Would you like another run? (y/n) y
Operations are:
    Addition
    Subtraction
    Multiplication by a scalar

operation (a, s, m): m
scalar: 3

Matrix dimensions:
    Number of Rows: 3
    Number of Cols: 3

Matrix 1:
  Row 1
    Value in column 1: -4
    Value in column 2: -1
    Value in column 3: 1
  Row 2
    Value in column 1: 11
    Value in column 2: 7.9
    Value in column 3: .5
  Row 3
    Value in column 1: 2
    Value in column 2: 6
    Value in column 3: -2


  -1.20000E1       -3.00000        3.00000
   3.30000E1        2.37000E1      1.50000
    6.00000         1.80000E1     -6.00000
Would you like another run? (y/n) n
```

Program Listing:

```pascal
program MatrixOperations(input,output);
const   MaxRows = 3;
        MaxCols = 3;

var   matrix : array[1..2 , 1..MaxRows , 1..MaxCols] of real;
      NumRows, NumCols : integer;
      operation : char;
      scalar : real;
```

124

```
{$I ReadInt }
{$I ReadReal }
{$I NotAgain }


procedure ReadData;
var  NumMatrices, h, j, k : integer;

begin
  NumMatrices:= 2;
  writeln('Operations are:');
  writeln('    Addition');
  writeln('    Subtraction');
  writeln('    Multiplication by a scalar');
  writeln;
  repeat
    write('operation (a, s, m): ');
    readln(operation);
  until operation in ['a','s','m','A','S','M'];
  if operation in ['m','M'] then
    begin
      NumMatrices:= 1;
      repeat
        write('scalar: ')
      until ReadReal(scalar);
    end;
  writeln;
  writeln('Matrix dimensions:');
  repeat
    write('      Number of Rows: ')
  until ReadInt(NumRows, 1, MaxRows);
  repeat
    write('      Number of Cols: ')
  until ReadInt(NumCols, 1, MaxCols);
  writeln;
  for h:=1 to NumMatrices do
    begin
      writeln('Matrix ',h,':');
      for j:=1 to NumRows do
        begin
          writeln('  Row ',j);
          for k:=1 to NumCols do
            begin
              repeat
                write('    Value in column ',k,': ')
              until ReadReal(matrix[h,j,k]);
              if operation in ['m','M'] then
                matrix[h,j,k]:= matrix[h,j,k] * scalar
              else
                if (operation in ['s','S']) and (h=2) then
                  matrix[h,j,k]:= -matrix[h,j,k]
            end
        end;
      writeln
    end
end; { procedure ReadData }


procedure AddMatrices;
var  j, k : integer;
```

```
begin
  for j:=1 to NumRows do
    for k:=1 to NumRows do
      matrix[1,j,k]:= matrix[1,j,k] + matrix[2,j,k]
end; { procedure AddMatrices }


procedure PrintResults;
var  j, k : integer;

begin
  for j:=1 to NumRows do
    begin
      for k:=1 to NumCols do
        write(matrix[1,j,k]:13);
      writeln
    end
end; { procedure PrintResults }


begin  { main }
  writeln; write('Matrix Addition, Subtraction, ');
  writeln('and Scalar Multiplication');
  writeln;
  repeat
    ReadData;
    if not (operation in ['m','M']) then
      AddMatrices;
    writeln;
    PrintResults;
  until NotAgain;
end.
```

46
Matrix Multiplication

This program multiplies two matrices. The first matrix is multiplied by the second. You must input the elements of each matrix.

In order for this operation to be performed, the number of rows in the first matrix must equal the number of columns in the second matrix.

Program Notes

You must specify the size of every matrix before you enter the data points. Presently, you are limited to no more than ten rows and ten columns in any matrix. These maxima are set by the constants "MaxRows" and "MaxCols."

Example:

Multiply matrix 1 by matrix 2.

$$1 \begin{cases} 2 & -1 & 4 & 1 & 2 \\ 1 & 0 & 1 & 2 & -1 \\ 2 & 3 & -1 & 0 & -2 \end{cases}$$

$$2 \begin{cases} -2 & -1 & 2 \\ 0 & 2 & 1 \\ -1 & 1 & 4 \\ 3 & 0 & -1 \\ 2 & 1 & 2 \end{cases}$$

Run:

```
Matrix Multiplication

Matrix 1 dimensions
   Number of rows: 3
   Number of columns: 5

Matrix 2 dimensions
   Number of rows: 5
   Number of columns: 3

Matrix 1
   Row 1
      Value in column 1: 2
      Value in column 2: -1
      Value in column 3: 4
      Value in column 4: 1
      Value in column 5: 2
   Row 2
      Value in column 1: 1
      Value in column 2: 0
```

```
            Value in column 3: 1
            Value in column 4: 2
            Value in column 5: -1
      Row 3
            Value in column 1: 2
            Value in column 2: 3
            Value in column 3: -1
            Value in column 4: 0
            Value in column 5: -2

   Matrix 2
      Row 1
            Value in column 1: -2
            Value in column 2: -1
            Value in column 3: 2
      Row 2
            Value in column 1: 0
            Value in column 2: 2
            Value in column 3: 1
      Row 3
            Value in column 1: -1
            Value in column 2: 1
            Value in column 3: 4
      Row 4
            Value in column 1: 3
            Value in column 2: 0
            Value in column 3: -1
      Row 5
            Value in column 1: 2
            Value in column 2: 1
            Value in column 3: 2


      -1.00000        2.00000      2.20000E1
       1.00000       -1.00000      2.00000
      -7.00000        1.00000     -1.00000
Would you like another run? (y/n) n
```

Program Listing:

```pascal
program MatrixMultiplication(input,output);
const   MaxRows = 10;
        MaxCols = 10;

type    RowOrCol = (rows,cols);

var     matrix : array[1..2 , 1..MaxRows , 1..MaxCols] of real
        size : array[1..2 , rows..cols] of integer;


{$I ReadInt }
{$I ReadReal }
{$I NotAgain }


procedure ReadData;
var  low, high, h, j, k : integer;

begin
   low:= 1;
```

```
    high:= MaxRows;
    for h:=1 to 2 do
      begin
        writeln('Matrix ',h,' dimensions');
        repeat
          write('  Number of rows: ')
        until ReadInt(size[h,rows], low, high);
        repeat
          write('  Number of columns: ')
        until ReadInt(size[h,cols], 1, MaxCols);
        low:= size[h,cols];
        high:= low;
        writeln;
      end;
    writeln;
    for h:=1 to 2 do
      begin
        writeln('Matrix ',h);
        for j:=1 to size[h,rows] do
          begin
            writeln('  Row ',j);
            for k:=1 to size[h,cols] do
              repeat
                write('    Value in column ',k,': ')
              until ReadReal(matrix[h,j,k])
          end;
        writeln
      end
end; { procedure ReadData }


procedure PrintResults;
var  h, j, k : integer;
     sum : real;

begin
  for h:=1 to size[1,rows] do
    begin
      for j:=1 to size[2,cols] do
        begin
          sum:= 0;
          for k:=1 to size[2,rows] do
            sum:= sum + matrix[1,h,k] * matrix[2,k,j];
          write(sum:13)
        end;
      writeln
    end
end; { procedure PrintResults }


begin  { main }
  writeln; writeln('Matrix Multiplication');
  writeln;
  repeat
    ReadData;
    writeln;
    PrintResults
  until NotAgain
end.
```

47
Matrix Inversion

This program inverts a square matrix. The inversion is performed by a modified Gauss-Jordan elimination method.

Program Notes

The program will accept a square matrix up to 10×10. To set a larger or smaller maximum size, change the constant "MaxOrder."

Example:

Invert matrix A.

$$A \begin{cases} 3 & 5 & -1 & -4 \\ 1 & 4 & -0.7 & -3 \\ 0 & -2 & 0 & 1 \\ -2 & 6 & 0 & 0.3 \end{cases}$$

Run:

```
Matrix Inversion

Dimension of matrix: 4

Row 1
  Value in column 1: 3
  Value in column 2: 5
  Value in column 3: -1
  Value in column 4: -4
Row 2
  Value in column 1: 1
  Value in column 2: 4
  Value in column 3: -.7
  Value in column 4: -3
Row 3
  Value in column 1: 0
  Value in column 2: -2
  Value in column 3: 0
  Value in column 4: 1
Row 4
  Value in column 1: -2
  Value in column 2: 6
  Value in column 3: 0
  Value in column 4: .3

    6.54391E-1   -9.34844E-1   -1.91218E-1    1.41643E-2
    1.98300E-1   -2.83286E-1   -1.03399E-1    1.55807E-1
    3.68272E-1     -1.95467      -4.26346    -4.24929E-1
    3.96601E-1   -5.66572E-1    7.93201E-1    3.11615E-1
```

Program Listing:

```pascal
program MatrixInversion(input,output);
const  MaxOrder = 10;

type  MatrixType = array[1..MaxOrder , 1..MaxOrder] of real;

var  Matrix, SecondMatrix : MatrixType;
     order : integer;
     error : boolean;


{$I ReadInt }
{$I ReadReal }


procedure ReadData;
var  j, k : integer;

begin
  repeat
    write('Dimension of matrix: ')
  until ReadInt(order, 1, MaxOrder);
  writeln;
  for j:=1 to order do
    begin
      writeln('Row ',j:0);
      for k:=1 to order do
        begin
          repeat
            write('  Value in column ',k:0,': ')
          until ReadReal(matrix[j,k]);
          if j=k then SecondMatrix[k,k]:=1
          else SecondMatrix[j,k]:=0
        end
    end
end;  { procedure ReadData }


procedure invert;
var  h, j, k, exchange : integer;
     hold, InvertedElement, NegativeElement : real;

begin
  for h:=1 to order do
    begin
      error:= true;
      for j:=h to order do
        if matrix[j,h]<>0 then
          begin
            error:= false;
            exchange:= j;
            j:= order
          end;
      if error then
        begin
          writeln('Matrix is not invertible');
          h:= order
        end
      else
```

```
          begin
            for j:=1 to order do
              begin
                hold:= matrix[h,j];
                matrix[h,j]:= matrix[exchange,j];
                matrix[exchange,j]:= hold;
                hold:= SecondMatrix[h,j];
                SecondMatrix[h,j]:= SecondMatrix[exchange,j];
                SecondMatrix[exchange,j]:= hold
              end;
            InvertedElement:= 1 / matrix[h,h];
            for j:=1 to order do
              begin
                matrix[h,j]:= InvertedElement * matrix[h,j];
                SecondMatrix[h,j]:= InvertedElement * SecondMatrix[h,j]
              end;
            for j:=1 to order do
              if j<>h then
                begin
                  NegativeElement:= -matrix[j,h];
                  for k:=1 to order do
                    begin
                      matrix[j,k]:=matrix[j,k] + NegativeElement *
                                                   matrix[h,k];
                      SecondMatrix[j,k]:= SecondMatrix[j,k] +
                                    NegativeElement * SecondMatrix[h,k]
                    end;
                end;
          end { else (if not error) }
      end { for h }
end; { procedure invert }


procedure PrintResults;
var  j, k : integer;

begin
  for j:=1 to order do
    begin
      for k:=1 to order do
        write(SecondMatrix[j,k]:13);
      writeln
    end
end; { procedure PrintResults }


begin   { main }
  writeln; writeln('Matrix Inversion');
  writeln;
  ReadData;
  Invert;
  writeln;
  if not error then
    PrintResults
end.
```

48
Permutations and Combinations

This program calculates the number of permutations and combinations possible for a given total number of objects, taken a certain number at a time. You provide the total and the size of the subgroup.

Examples:

How many permutations and combinations can be made of the 26 letters of the alphabet, taking five at a time?
How many different ways can twelve people sit on a park bench if there is only room for two at a time?

Run:

```
Permutations and Combinations

Total number of objects: 26
Size of subgroup: 5
 7.89360E6 permutations
 6.57800E4 combinations
Would you like another run? (y/n) y

Total number of objects: 12
Size of subgroup: 2
 1.32000E2 permutations
 6.60000E1 combinations
Would you like another run? (y/n) n
```

Program Listing:

```
program PermutationsAndCombinations(input,output);
const  MaxPerms = 9.9E36;

var  NumObjects, R : integer;
     Overflow : boolean;

{$I ReadInt }
{$I NotAgain }

procedure InputData;
begin
  repeat
    write('Total number of objects: ')
  until ReadInt(NumObjects, 1, maxint);
  repeat
    write('Size of subgroup: ');
  until ReadInt(R, 1, NumObjects);
  Overflow:=false;
end;  { procedure InputData }
```

```
function CalcPandC:boolean;
var  perms, CombFactor : real;
     i : integer;

begin
  perms:= 1;
  CombFactor:= 1;
  for i:=NumObjects-R+1 to NumObjects do
    if MaxPerms / i >= perms then
      perms:= perms * i
    else
      begin
        writeln('Number of permutations exceeds computer capacity');
        Overflow:= true;
        i:= NumObjects
      end;
  if not Overflow then
    begin
      for i:=2 to R do
        CombFactor:=CombFactor * i;
      writeln(perms:0,' permutations');
      writeln(perms/CombFactor:0,' combinations');
    end;
  CalcPandC:= not Overflow
end; { function CalcP&C }

begin  { main }
  writeln; writeln('Permutations and Combinations');
  repeat
    repeat
      writeln;
      InputData
    until CalcPandC;
  until NotAgain;
end.
```

49
Mann-Whitney *U* Test

This program performs the Mann-Whitney *U* test on samples from two populations.

Program Notes

The program limits you to samples of 25 or less. To increase or decrease this maximum, change the variable "MaxSizes." Since one variable controls the size of both samples, the samples must be of equal size.

Example:

A group of ten women and a group of ten men were asked to rate the flavor of a frozen TV dinner on a scale of one to ten. The table below lists the scores. Count the number of times the women's scores are lower than the men's, and vice versa.

Women	1	3	4	3	6	8	9	7	8	4
Men	7	9	8	5	10	9	10	6	5	2

Run:

```
Mann-Whitney U Test

Sample 1:
  Size: 10
    Data 1: 1
    Data 2: 3
    Data 3: 4
    Data 4: 3
    Data 5: 6
    Data 6: 8
    Data 7: 9
    Data 8: 7
    Data 9: 8
    Data 10: 4
Sample 2:
  Size: 10
    Data 1: 7
    Data 2: 9
    Data 3: 8
    Data 4: 5
    Data 5: 10
    Data 6: 9
    Data 7: 10
    Data 8: 6
    Data 9: 5
    Data 10: 2
First sample preceding, U = 70
Second sample preceding, U = 30

Would you like another run? (y/n) n
```

Program Listing:

```
program MannWhitneyUTest(input,output);
const   MaxSize = 25;
        MaxReal = 9.9E36;

type    IntArray = array[1..2] of integer;
        RealArray = array[1..2] of real;

var     size, sum : IntArray;
        subtract : RealArray;
        sample : array[1..2 , 0..MaxSize] of real;


{$I ReadInt }
{$I ReadReal}
{$I NotAgain}


procedure ReadData;
var  h, j, k : integer;
     hold : real;

begin
  for h:=1 to 2 do
    begin
      writeln('Sample ',h,':');
      repeat
        write('  Size: ')
      until ReadInt(size[h], 1, MaxSize);
      for j:=1 to size[h] do
        repeat
          write('    Data ',j,': ')
        until ReadReal(sample[h, j-1]);
    end;
  for h:=1 to 2 do
    begin
      for j:=0 to size[h]-2 do
        for k:=0 to size[h]-j-2 do
          if sample[h, k] > sample[h, k+1] then
            begin
              hold:= sample[h, k];
              sample[h, k]:= sample[h, k+1];
              sample[h, k+1]:= hold
            end;
      sample[h, size[h]]:= MaxReal
    end;
end;  { procedure ReadData }


procedure FindValues;
var  j, k, m, precedes, lookahead : integer;

begin
  for j:=1 to 2 do
    begin
      if j=1 then m:=2
      else  m:=1;
      precedes:=0;
      sum[j]:=0;
      subtract[j]:= 0;
```

```
          for k:=0 to size[m]-1 do
            begin
              while sample[j, precedes] <= sample[m, k] do
                begin
                  if sample[j,precedes] = sample[m,k] then
                    begin
                      lookahead:= k;
                      while sample[m,lookahead] = sample[j,precedes] do
                        begin
                          subtract[j]:= subtract[j] + 0.5;
                          lookahead:= lookahead + 1
                        end
                    end;
                  precedes:= precedes + 1
                end;
              sum[j]:= sum[j] + precedes
            end;
          sum[j]:= sum[j] - trunc(subtract[j] + 0.5)
      end
end; { procedure FindUValues }


procedure PrintResults;
begin
  write('First sample preceding, U = ',sum[1]);
  if odd(trunc(subtract[1] * 2)) then write('.5');
  writeln;
  write('Second sample preceding, U = ',sum[2]);
  if odd(trunc(subtract[2] * 2)) then write('.5');
  writeln;
end; { procedure PrintResults }


begin   { main }
  writeln; writeln('Mann-Whitney U-Test');
  writeln;
  repeat
    ReadData;
    FindValues;
    PrintResults;
    writeln;
  until NotAgain
end.
```

50
Mean, Variance, and Standard Deviation

This program calculates the arithmetic mean, variance, and standard deviation of grouped or ungrouped data. The data may represent the entire population or a sample of the population.

Examples:

Ten people in a hotel lobby are aged 87, 53, 35, 42, 9, 48, 51, 60, 39, and 44 years. What is the mean, standard deviation, and variance of the ages of all the people in the hotel, if the people in the lobby represent a sample?

Find the mean, variance, and standard deviation of the ages of the cream cheese on a market shelf. The table below lists the age distribution of 50 packages of cream cheese. Assume that the data represent the store's entire inventory.

Calculate the mean, variance, and standard deviation of the ages of the cream cheese if the data are only a sample of the total population.

Age	1	2	3	4	5	6
Quantity	15	10	9	6	7	3

Cream Cheese

Run:

```
Mean, Variance, Standard Deviation

Which method: P(opulation) or S(ample), enter letter: s
Which kind of data: G(rouped) or U(ngrouped), enter letter: u
Number of observations: 10
Item 1: 87
Item 2: 53
Item 3: 35
Item 4: 42
Item 5: 9
Item 6: 48
Item 7: 51
Item 8: 60
Item 9: 39
Item 10: 44


      MEAN     VARIANCE    STD. DEV.
   46.8000     389.733      19.7417

Would you like another run? (y/n) y

Which method: P(opulation) or S(ample), enter letter: p
Which kind of data: G(rouped) or U(ngrouped), enter letter: g
Number of observations: 6
Item 1: 1
frequency: 15
Item 2: 2
frequency: 10
```

```
Item 3: 3
frequency: 9
Item 4: 4
frequency: 6
Item 5: 5
frequency: 7
Item 6: 6
frequency: 3

        MEAN      VARIANCE    STD. DEV.
       2.78000    2.57160     1.60362

Would you like another run? (y/n) y

Which method: P(opulation) or S(ample), enter letter: s
Which kind of data: G(rouped) or U(ngrouped), enter letter: g
Number of observations: 6
Item 1: 1
frequency: 15
Item 2: 2
frequency: 10
Item 3: 3
frequency: 9
Item 4: 4
frequency: 6
Item 5: 5
frequency: 7
Item 6: 6
frequency: 3

        MEAN      VARIANCE    STD. DEV.
       2.78000    2.62408     1.61990

Would you like another run? (y/n) n
```

Program Listing:

```pascal
program MeanVarStanDev(input, output);
uses transcendentals; { omit this line if not using Apple Pascal }
type
   CharSet = set of char;
var
   sample, grouped: boolean;
   value, sum, SumSqrs, variance: real;
   NumItems, NumSamps, item, frequency: integer;

{$I ReadReal}
{$I ReadInt}
{$I readlchar}
{$I NotAgain}
```

```
begin { main }
  writeln('Mean, Variance, Standard Deviation');
  repeat
    writeln;
    write('Which method: P(opulation) or S(ample), enter letter: ');
    sample := read1char(['p', 's']) = 's';
    write('Which kind of data: G(rouped) or U(ngrouped), enter letter: ');
    grouped := read1char(['g', 'u']) = 'g';
    repeat
      write('Number of observations: ')
    until ReadInt(NumItems, 2, maxint);
    frequency := 1;
    NumSamps := 0;
    sum := 0.0;
    SumSqrs := 0.0;
    for item := 1 to NumItems do
      begin
        repeat
          write('Item ', item:0, ': ')
        until ReadReal(value);
        if grouped then
          repeat
            write('frequency: ')
          until ReadInt(frequency, 1, maxint);
        NumSamps := NumSamps + frequency;
        sum := sum + value * frequency;
        SumSqrs := SumSqrs + sqr(value) * frequency
      end;
    writeln;

    writeln('MEAN':12, 'VARIANCE':12, 'STD. DEV.':12);
    variance := SumSqrs - sqr(sum) / NumSamps;
    if sample then
      variance := variance / (NumSamps - 1)
    else
      variance := variance / NumSamps;
    writeln(sum / NumSamps:12:6, variance:12:6, sqrt(variance):12:6);
    writeln
  until NotAgain
end.
```

51
Geometric Mean and Deviation

This program computes the geometric mean and standard deviation of a set of data.

Example:

Find the geometric mean and standard deviation of 3, 5, 8, 3, 7, 2.

Run:

```
Geometric Mean and Deviation

Number of observations: 6
item 1: 3
item 2: 5
item 3: 8
item 4: 3
item 5: 7
item 6: 2

Geometric mean =      4.14068
Geometric deviation =      1.72369

Would you like another run? (y/n) n
```

Program Listing:

```
program GeometricMean(input, output);
uses transcendentals; { omit this line if not using Apple Pascal }
var
  NumObs, obs: integer;
  item, root, ProdRoots, SumDevTerms: real;

{$I ReadInt}
{$I ReadReal}
{$I RealRaise}
{$I NotAgain}
```

```
begin { main }
  writeln('Geometric Mean and Deviation');
  repeat
    writeln;
    repeat
      write('Number of observations: ')
    until ReadInt(NumObs, 2, maxint);
    root := 1 / NumObs;
    ProdRoots := 1.0;
    SumDevTerms := 0.0;
    for obs := 1 to NumObs do
      begin
        repeat
          write('item ', obs:0, ': ')
        until ReadReal(item);
        ProdRoots := ProdRoots * RealRaise(item, root);
        SumDevTerms := SumDevTerms + sqr(ln(item))
      end;
    writeln;
    writeln('Geometric mean = ', ProdRoots:12:6);
    writeln('Geometric deviation = ',
            exp(sqrt(SumDevTerms / (NumObs - 1)
                - (NumObs / (NumObs - 1) * sqr(ln(ProdRoots)))))):12:6);
    writeln
  until NotAgain
end.
```

52
Binomial Distribution

This program calculates the probability of obtaining a given number of successes in a given number of Bernoulli trials. You must know the probability of success on a single trial.

Examples:

What is the probability of getting three heads in five tosses of a fair coin?
    What is the probability that in five rolls of a fair die, a one (1) appears twice?

Run:

```
Binomial Distribution

Number of trials: 5
Exact number of successes: 3
Probabiity of success: .5
Probability of 3 successes in 5 trials =  0.312500
Would you like another run? (y/n) y

Number of trials: 5
Exact number of successes: 2
Probabiity of success: .1666667
Probability of 2 successes in 5 trials =  0.160751
Would you like another run? (y/n) n
```

Program Listing:

```
program BinomialDistribution(input,output);
uses transcend;  { omit if not using Apple Pascal  }

var  M : array[1..3] of real;
     trials, successes : integer;
     probability : real;

{$I ReadReal }
{$I ReadInt }
{$I NotAgain }

function FactLog(arg : integer) : real;
var  j : integer;
     factorial : real;

begin
  factorial:= 1;
  for j:=2 to arg do
    factorial:= factorial * j;
  FactLog:= ln(factorial)
end; { function FactLog }
```

```
procedure ReadData;

begin
  repeat
    write('Number of trials: ')
  until ReadInt(trials, 1, 34);
  M[1]:= FactLog(trials);
  repeat
    write('Exact number of successes: ')
  until ReadInt(successes, 1, trials);
  M[2]:= FactLog(successes);
  repeat
    write('Probabiity of success: ')
  until ReadReal(probability) and (probability>0) and (probability<1);
  M[3]:= FactLog(trials - successes);
end; { procedure ReadData }


procedure PrintResults;
var  r : real;

begin
  r:= exp(M[1] - M[2] - M[3] + successes * ln(probability) +
       (trials - successes) * ln(1 - probability));
  writeln('Probability of ',successes,' successes in ',trials,
          ' trials = ',r);
end; { procedure PrintResults }


begin  { main }
  writeln; writeln('Binomial Distribution');
  repeat
    writeln;
    ReadData;
    PrintResults
  until NotAgain
end.
```

53
Poisson Distribution

Using the Poisson distribution, this program calculates the probability of a event occurring a given number of times. You must know the expected frequency of the event.

Example:

Two thousand people are injected with a serum. The probability of any one person having a bad reaction is .001. Thus we can expect that two $(0.001 \cdot 2000 = 2)$ individuals will suffer a bad reaction. What is the probability that four people will have bad reactions? Only one person?

Run:

```
Poisson Distribution

Expected frequency: 2
Test frequency: 4
Probability of 4 occurances =   9.02235E-2
Would you like another run? (y/n) y
Expected frequency: 2
Test frequency: 1
Probability of 1 occurances =   2.70671E-1
Would you like another run? (y/n) n
```

Program Listing:

```
program PoissonDistribution(input,output);
uses transcend;  { Omit if not using Apple Pascal }
var   test, expect : integer;
      results : real;

{$I NotAgain }
{$I ReadInt }


procedure ReadData;
begin
  repeat
    write('Expected frequency: ')
  until ReadInt(expect, 1, maxint);
  repeat
    write('Test frequency: ');
  until ReadInt(test, 1, maxint);
end; { procedure ReadData }
```

```
function factorial(x:integer) : real;
var   j : integer;
      fact : real;

begin
  fact:= 1.0;
  for j:=2 to x do
    fact:= fact * j;
  factorial:= fact
end; { function factorial }


procedure CalculateProbability;
begin
  results:= exp(-expect +test * ln(expect) - ln(factorial(test)));;
  writeln('Probability of ',test,' occurances = ',
          results)
end; { procedure CalculateProbability }


begin { main }
  writeln('Poisson Distribution');
  writeln;
  repeat
    ReadData;
    CalculateProbability
  until NotAgain
end.
```

54
Normal Distribution

This program calculates the probability and frequency of given values on a standard normal distribution curve. You can use non-standard variables if you know the mean and standard deviation.

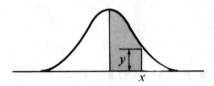

Standard Normal Distribution

The shaded area represents the probability of x. y corresponds to the frequency of x.
    The normal probability is approximated using the following formula:

$$probability = 1 - r(a_1t + a_2t^2 + a_3t^3) + \epsilon(x)$$

$$\begin{aligned}where: \quad a_1 &= 0.4361836 \\ a_2 &= -0.1201676 \\ a_3 &= 0.9372980 \\ r &= (e^{-x^2/2})(2\pi)^{-\frac{1}{2}} \\ t &= (1 + 0.3326x)^{-1} \\ |\epsilon(x)| &< 10^{-5}\end{aligned}$$

Example:

The mean weight of the male students at a college is 150 pounds. The standard deviation is 15 pounds. If the weights are normally distributed, what is the probability that a student weighs between 150 and 180 pounds? Between 130 and 150 pounds?

Run:

```
Normal Distribution

Using a non-standard variable? (y/n) y
mean: 150
standard deviation: 15
x = ? 180
Frequency =  0.053991
Probability =  0.977241
Another x value? y
x = ? 130
Frequency =  0.164010
Probability =  0.908798
Another x value? n

Would you like another run? (y/n) n
```

Program Listing:

```
program NormalDistribution(input,output);
uses transcend;  { Omit if not using Apple Pascal }
var  v : char;
     mean, sd, XValue, probability : real;



{$I NotAgain }
{$I IntRaise }



procedure ReadData;
begin
  sd:= 1;
  mean:= 0;
  repeat
    write('Using a non-standard variable? (y/n) ');
    readln(v)
  until v in ['y','n','N','Y'];
  if v in ['y','Y'] then
    begin
      write('mean: ');
      readln(mean);
      write('standard deviation: ');
      readln(sd);
    end
end;  { procedure ReadData }



procedure calculate;
var  frequency, t, multiplier : real;
     negative : boolean;

begin
  write('x = ? ');
  readln(XValue);
  XValue:= abs((XValue - mean) / sd);
  frequency:= exp(-(XValue * XValue) / 2) / 2.5066282746;
  negative:= XValue < 0;
  XValue:= 1 / (1 + 0.33267 * abs(XValue));
  multiplier:= 0.4361836 * XValue - 0.120167 * (XValue * XValue) +
                                  0.937298 * IntRaise(XValue,3);
  probability:= 1 - frequency * multiplier;
  if negative then probability:= 1 - probability;
  writeln('Frequency = ',frequency:1:6);
  writeln('Probability = ',probability:1:6);
end;  { procedure calculate }



begin  { main }
  writeln; writeln('Normal Distribution');
  writeln;
  repeat
    ReadData;
    repeat
      calculate;
      write('Another x value? ');
      readln(v)
    until  v in ['n','N'];
  until NotAgain
end.
```

55
Chi-Square Distribution

This program calculates the percentile and tail-end values for points on a chi-square (x^2) distribution. You must provide the value of X^2 and the degrees of freedom.

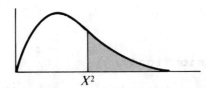

Chi-Square Distribution

The shaded area represents the tail-end value of X^2.
   The X^2 distribution function is calculated using the following formulas:

$$\text{with } v \text{ odd, tail-end value} = 1 - \frac{(X^2)(v+1)/2 \cdot e^{-x^2/2}}{1 \cdot 3 \cdot 5 \cdot \ldots v} \cdot \left(\frac{2}{X^2 \pi}\right)^{1/2} \cdot Z$$

$$\text{with } v \text{ even, tail-end value} = 1 - \frac{(X^2)v/2 \cdot e^{-x^2/2}}{2 \cdot 4 \cdot \ldots v} \cdot Z$$

where: v = degrees of freedom

$$Z = 1 + \sum_{m=1}^{\infty} \frac{(X^2)^m}{(v+2) \cdot (v+4) \cdot \ldots (v+2m)}$$

Since the summation cannot actually proceed to infinity in practice, summation stops when the next term is less than 10^{-7}.

Example:

A group of 168 people complained of insomnia. In a study, 54 were given a new sleep-inducing drug and the remainder received a placebo. When the study was complete, the X^2 statistic was computed as 2.571108 with one degree of freedom. What is the tail-end value? What is the percentile?

Run:

```
Chi-square Distribution
Degrees of freedom (0 ends program): 1
Chi-square value: 2.571108


Tail end value=  0.108832

Percentile=  0.891168

Degrees of freedom (0 ends program): 0
```

Program Listing:

```pascal
program ChiSquareDistribution(input, output);
uses transcendentals; { omit this line if not using Apple Pascal }
const
  pi = 3.14159265358979;
var
  df, i: integer;
  ChiSqr, numerator, denominator, ParityFactor, sum, term, percentile: real;

{$I ReadInt}
{$I ReadReal}
{$I RealRaise}

begin { main }
  writeln('Chi-square Distribution');
  repeat
    write('Degrees of freedom (0 ends program): ')
  until ReadInt(df, 0, maxint);
  while df <> 0 do
    begin
      repeat
        write('Chi-square value: ')
      until ReadReal(ChiSqr);
      writeln;

      denominator := 1;
      for i := 1 to df do
        if odd(i) then
          denominator := denominator * i;

      numerator := RealRaise(ChiSqr, (df + 1) div 2)
                 * exp(- ChiSqr / 2) / denominator;

      if odd(df) then
        ParityFactor := sqrt(2 / ChiSqr / pi)
      else
        ParityFactor := 1;

      sum := 1;
      term := 1;
      repeat
        df := df + 2;
        term := term * ChiSqr / df;
        sum := sum + term
      until term < 1.0E-7;

      percentile:=ParityFactor*numerator*sum;
      writeln;
      writeln('Tail end value= ',1-percentile:8:6);
      writeln;
      writeln('Percentile= ',percentile:8:6);
      writeln;
      repeat
        write('Degrees of freedom (0 ends program): ')
      until ReadInt(df, 0, maxint)
    end
end.
```

56
Chi-Square Test

The chi-square test in statistics tests the compatibility of observed frequencies with the expected or theoretical frequencies. For example, suppose we are testing whether a die is fair or biased. We throw the die 60 times, recording the result each time. If the die is fair, we would expect that each of the six sides would come up close to ten times during the test. But we know that events do not always correspond to theoretical expectations. The chi-square test provides the means of determining whether the observed and theoretical results are so divergent that the die cannot be considered fair.

Chi-square is defined as follows:

$$x^2 = \sum_{I=1}^{K} \frac{(O_I - E_I)^2}{E_I}$$

where O represented the observed frequencies and E the expected frequencies. Statisticians have determined what value (the "5% critical value") the chi-square must be below in order that we be 95% positive that two results are compatible. This program tests whether the actual results fall within that level of confidence. It also employs Yates's correction (which some statisticians prefer and some dislike) to test the results. The chi-square formula with Yates's correction is

$$x^2 = \sum_{I=1}^{K} \left(\frac{|O_I - E_I| - 0.5}{E_I} \right)^2$$

The program also tests whether the results are too good (below the 95% critical value), which makes clinical workers suspicious of the results.

The program first asks if the expected frequency is a constant. In the above example, each face of the die is expected to appear 10 times, so the answer is "Yes" and you would enter 10 as the constant. The program then asks for the number of samples. In the above example, there are 6 samples. You then enter the observed frequencies one by one. If the expected frequencies are not constant, the program will ask for each pair of observed and expected frequencies.

The program will then calculate the chi-square statistics, both with and without Yates's correction, and print them out, indicating the degrees of freedom. It then tests each statistic against the 5% and 95% critical values, and prints out the results.

Example:

Suppose the results of the 60 throws of the die in the above example are as follows:

Face	Expected	Actual
1	10	9
2	10	8
3	10	12
4	10	10
5	10	13
6	10	8

What are the results of the chi-square test for this data? Can the die be considered fair?

Answer: The die can be considered fair.

Run:

```
Chi-Square
Is the expected frequency constant? (y/n) y
Enter constant expected frequency: 10
```

```
Number of samples: 6
Sample 1 observed: 9
Sample 2 observed: 8
Sample 3 observed: 12
Sample 4 observed: 10
Sample 5 observed: 13
Sample 6 observed: 8
Degrees of freedom = 5
Chi-square =  2.20
Chi-square with Yates' correction =  1.35
The 5% critical value of Chi-square is  11.071
therefore the hypothesis is not
rejected at the 5% critical value
```

Practice Problems:

1. A student in a genetics class is performing an experiment to test classical Mendelian theory. That theory predicts that certain biological characteristics should appear in the species under review in the ratios 900:300:300:100. In the 1,600 samples which the student takes, they appear 904, 297, 302, and 97 times, respectively. Are these results compatible with orthodox Mendelian theory?

Answer: The unadjusted chi-square result is 0.151111111, and with Yates's correction that result is 0.104444444. The 5% critical value for three degrees of freedom is 7.8147, so the results are compatible. However, the 95% critical value is 0.35185, so either with or without Yates's correction, the results are "too good," and the instructor must view the student's experiment with suspicion.

2. A Las Vegas pit boss noticed that a particular roulette wheel seemed to be coming up red more often than black. He kept track of the next 1,000 spins; red came up 546 times, and black 454 times. Is the wheel biased?

Answer: The chi-square without Yates's correction is 8.46400001, and with it is 8.28100001. The 5% critical value is 3.8415, and the hypothesis is therefore rejected. The pit boss should junk that roulette wheel immediately.

Program Listing:

```pascal
program ChiSquare(input, output);
uses transcendentals;
var
  NumSamps, sample: integer;
  ConstFreq: boolean;
  observed, expected, ChiSqrSum, YatesSum, crit5, crit95: real;

{$I YesNotNo}
{$I ReadReal}
{$I ReadInt}

  procedure FindCriticalValues(DegFree: integer);
  var
    temp1, temp2: real;

    procedure vals(c5, c95: real);
    begin
      crit5 := c5;
      crit95 := c95
```

```
    end; { vals }

    procedure LookUp(df: integer);
    begin
      case df of
        1: vals(3.8415, 0.003932);      2: vals(5.9915, 0.10259);
        3: vals(7.8127, 0.35185);       4: vals(9.4877, 0.71072);
        5: vals(11.071, 1.1455);        6: vals(12.529, 1.635);
        7: vals(14.067, 2.167);         8: vals(15.507, 2.733);
        9: vals(16.919, 3.325);        10: vals(18.307, 3.940);
       11: vals(19.675, 4.575);        12: vals(21.026, 5.226);
       13: vals(22.362, 5.892);        14: vals(23.685, 6.571);
       15: vals(24.996, 7.261);        16: vals(26.296, 7.962);
       17: vals(27.587, 8.672);        18: vals(28.869, 9.390);
       19: vals(30.140, 10.117);       20: vals(31.410, 10.851);
       21: vals(32.671, 11.591);       22: vals(33.924, 12.338);
       23: vals(35.173, 13.091);       24: vals(36.415, 13.848);
       25: vals(37.653, 14.611);       26: vals(38.885, 15.379);
       27: vals(40.113, 16.151);       28: vals(41.337, 16.928);
       29: vals(42.557, 17.708);       30: vals(43.773, 18.493)
      end; { case }
    end; { LookUp }

begin { FindCriticalValues }
  if DegFree > 100 then
    vals(123.342, 77.9295)
  else if DegFree = 100 then
    vals(124.342, 77.9295)
  else if DegFree > 30 then
    begin
      temp1 := 2 / (9 * DegFree);
      temp2 := temp1 * sqrt(temp1);
      temp1 := DegFree * (1 - temp1);
      vals(temp1 + 1.6449 * temp2, temp1 - 1.6449 * temp2)
    end
  else
    LookUp(DegFree);
  writeln('The 5% critical value of Chi-square is ', crit5:6:3);
end; { FindCriticalValues }

procedure GiveJudgement;
  begin
    if YatesSum > crit5 then
      begin
        writeln('therefore the hypothesis is');
        writeln('rejected at the 5% critical value.')
      end
    else if ChiSqrSum > crit5 then
      begin
        writeln('While the unadjusted Chi-square values');
        writeln('are unacceptable, those with Yates''');
        writeln('correction are not; therefore sample');
        writeln('sizes should be increased or substitute');
        writeln('multinomial distribution methods')
      end
```

153

```
        else if (ChiSqrSum < crit95) or (YatesSum < crit95) then
          begin
            writeln('Agreement is too good and should be examined');
            writeln('critically, because either with or without');
            writeln('Yates'' correction, the Chi-square value is');
            writeln('below the 95% critical value.')
          end
        else
          begin
            writeln('therefore the hypothesis is not');
            writeln('rejected at the 5% critical value')
          end
    end; { CriticalValue }

begin { main }
  writeln('Chi-Square');
  write('Is the expected frequency constant? (y/n) ');
  ConstFreq := YesNotNo;
  if ConstFreq then
    repeat
      write('Enter constant expected frequency: ')
    until ReadReal(expected);
  repeat
    write('Number of samples: ')
  until ReadInt(NumSamps, 2, maxint);

  ChiSqrSum := 0;
  YatesSum := 0;
  for sample := 1 to NumSamps do
    begin
      if not ConstFreq then
        repeat
          write('Sample ', sample:0, ' expected: ')
        until ReadReal(expected);
      repeat
        write('Sample ', sample:0, ' observed: ')
      until ReadReal(observed);
      ChiSqrSum := ChiSqrSum + sqr(observed - expected) / expected;
      YatesSum := YatesSum +
                  sqr(abs(observed - expected) - 0.5) / expected
    end; { for }

  writeln('Degrees of freedom = ', NumSamps - 1:0);
  writeln('Chi-square = ', ChiSqrSum:5:2);
  writeln('Chi-square with Yates'' correction = ', YatesSum:5:2);
  FindCriticalValues(NumSamps - 1);
  GiveJudgement
end.
```

References

Hoel. *Introduction to Mathematical Statistics,* 2nd. ed. New York: John Wiley, 1954.

Spiegel. *Statistics* (Schaum's series). New York: McGraw-Hill, 1961.

57
Student's *t*-distribution

This program calculates right-tail values for points on a *t*-distribution curve. You must provide the value of *t* and the degrees of freedom.

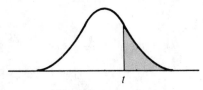

Student's *t*-distribution

The shaded area represents the right-tail value for *t*.
The right-tail value is approximated using the following formula:

$$\text{right-tail value} = \frac{1}{4}(1 + a_1 x + a_2 x^2 + a_3 x^3 + a_4 x^4)^{-4} + \epsilon(x)$$

$$\text{where: } a_1 = 0.196854$$
$$a_2 = 0.115194$$
$$a_3 = 0.000344$$
$$a_4 = 0.019527$$

$$x = \left(t^{2/3}\left(1 - \frac{2}{9d}\right) - \frac{7}{9} \right)\left(\frac{2}{9} + t^{4/3}\cdot\frac{2}{9d}\right)^{-1/2}$$

$$|\epsilon(x)| < 2.5 \cdot 10^{-4}$$

Examples:

What is the right-tail value when the *t*-value is 2.921 and there are 16 degrees of freedom?
What is the right-tail value when the *t*-value is 11.178 and there are 5 degrees of freedom?

Run:

```
T-distribution

T-value: 2.921
Degrees of freedom: 16

Right tail value =   4.87175E-3

Would you like another run? (y/n) y

T-value: 11.178
Degrees of freedom: 5

Right tail value =   2.07804E-4

Would you like another run? (y/n) n
```

Program Listing:

```pascal
program TDistribution(input,output);
uses transcend; { omit if not using Apple Pascal }
var
    Tvalue,
   RightTail:real;
   df:integer;


{$I ReadInt }
{$I ReadReal }
{$I RealRaise }
{$I IntRaise }
{$I NotAgain }


procedure ReadData;

begin
   repeat
     write('T-value: ' );
   until ReadReal(Tvalue);
   repeat
     write('Degrees of freedom: ');
   until ReadInt(df,1,maxint);
end;


procedure Calculate;

const
    a1 = 0.196854;
    a2 = 0.115194;
    a3 = 0.000344;
    a4 = 0.019527;

var
    temp,y : integer;
    L,x,
    factor1,factor2:real;
    LessThanOne:boolean;

begin
   y:= 1;
   Tvalue:= sqr(Tvalue);
   LessThanOne:= false;
   if Tvalue < 1.0 then
     begin
       Tvalue:=1/Tvalue;
       temp:= y;
       y:= df;
       df:= temp;
       LessThanZero:= true
     end;
   factor1:=2/(9 * y);
   factor2:=2/(9 * df);

   L:=abs(RealRaise(Tvalue,0.33333)*(1-factor2)-1+factor1) /
             sqrt((factor1+RealRaise(Tvalue ,0.666667)*factor2));
```

```
   if df < 4 then
     L:= L * (1 + 0.08 * IntRaise(L,4) /
                                IntRaise(df,3));

   x:= 0.25 / IntRaise((1 + L * (a1 + L * (a2 + L *
                                (a3 + L * a4)))),4);

   if LessThanZero then
     RightTail:= 1 - x
   else  RightTail:= x;
   writeln;
   writeln('Right tail value = ',RightTail)
end; { calculate }

begin { main }
   writeln;
   writeln('T-distribution');
   repeat
     writeln;
     ReadData;
     Calculate;
     writeln
   until NotAgain
end.
```

58
Student's *t*-distribution Test

This program calculates the *t*-statistic and degrees of freedom for Student's distribution. The calculations can be based on any one of three hypotheses.

The first hypothesis assumes that one population mean is equal to a given value. You must enter the elements of the sample and the value of the mean.

The remaining hypotheses compare two populations. In both tests the means of the two populations are equal, but the standard deviations may be equal or unequal. For these hypotheses you must enter the elements of each sample.

Program Notes

The maximum number of elements allowed for each sample is controlled by the constant "maxsize," which is currently set equal to 20.

Examples:

A sample of children's IQ's was taken, the results being 101, 99, 120, 79, 111, 98, 106, 112, 87, and 97. Calculate the *t*-statistic assuming the population mean is 100.

A second sample was taken, the results being 101, 95, 130, 150, 75, 79, 111, 100, 98, and 91. Calculate the *t*-statistic based on the hypothesis that the two samples have equal means and standard deviations.

Run:

```
Student's t-Distribution Test

Test 1:One population,one mean
Test 2:Means equal, standard deviations equal
Test 3:Means equal, standard deviations unequal

Choose hypothesis
Enter 1, 2 or 3 : 1

Sample size: 10
     Element 1: 101
     Element 2: 99
     Element 3: 120
     Element 4: 79
     Element 5: 111
     Element 6: 98
     Element 7: 106
     Element 8: 112
     Element 9: 87
     Element 10: 97
Population mean: 100

t-value =  2.61513E-1
9 degrees of freedom

Would you like another run? (y/n) y
```

158

```
Test 1:One population,one mean
Test 2:Means equal, standard deviations equal
Test 3:Means equal, standard deviations unequal

Choose hypothesis
Enter 1, 2 or 3 : 2

First sample:
  size: 10
    Element 1: 101
    Element 2: 99
    Element 3: 120
    Element 4: 79
    Element 5: 111
    Element 6: 98
    Element 7: 106
    Element 8: 112
    Element 9: 87
    Element 10: 97
Second Sample
  size: 10
    Element 1: 101
    Element 2: 95
    Element 3: 130
    Element 4: 150
    Element 5: 75
    Element 6: 79
    Element 7: 111
    Element 8: 10
    Element 9: 98
    Element 10: 91


t-value =  5.66246E-1
18 degrees of freedom

Would you like another run? (y/n) n
```

Program Listing:

```pascal
program tTest(input,output);
uses transcend;  { Omit if not using Apple Pascal }
const
  maxsize = 20;

var
  FirstSize,
  SecondSize,
  df:integer;
  a1,a2,value1,
  value2,tstat:real;


{$I ReadInt }
{$I Readreal }
{$I NotAgain }


procedure ReadElements(number:integer ; var a, value : real);
```

```
var
  sample,sum,
  squaresum:real;
  j:integer;

begin
  sum:=0;
  squaresum:=0;
  for j:= 1 to number do begin
     write('    Element ',j,': ');
     readln(sample);
     sum:=sum + sample;
     squaresum:=squaresum + sample*sample;
  end; { for }

  a:= sum/number;
  value:= (squaresum-(sum*sum)/number)/(number-1);

end; { readelements }


procedure FirstHypothesis;

var
   size:integer;
   mean:real;

begin
   repeat
     write('Sample size: ')
   until ReadInt(size,2,maxsize);

   ReadElements(size,a1,value1);

   repeat
     write('Population mean: ')
   until ReadReal(mean);

   tstat:=(a1-mean)*sqrt(size/value1);
   df:= size - 1
end;

procedure TwoSamples;

begin
   writeln('First sample:');
   repeat
     write('  size: ')
   until ReadInt(FirstSize,2,maxsize);
   ReadElements(FirstSize,a1,value1);
   writeln('Second Sample');
   repeat
     write('  size: ')
   until ReadInt(SecondSize,2,maxsize);
   ReadElements(SecondSize,a2,value2)

end;

procedure SecondHypothesis;

var
   temp1:real;
```

160

```
begin
    TwoSamples;
    temp1:= (a1-a2)/sqrt(1/FirstSize + 1/SecondSize);
    df:= FirstSize+SecondSize - 2;
    tstat:=temp1/sqrt((((FirstSize-1)*value1+(SecondSize-1)*value2) /
                                                       df);
end;


procedure ThirdHypothesis;

var
    fract1,fract2:real;

begin
    TwoSamples;
    fract1:= value1/FirstSize;
    fract2:= value2/SecondSize;
    df:=round(sqr(fract1+fract2)/(sqr(fract1)/(FirstSize+1) +
                           sqr(fract2)/(SecondSize+1)) - 2);
    tstat:= (a1 - a2) / sqrt(fract1 + fract2);
end;


procedure Menu;

var
    hypothesis:integer;

begin
    writeln('Test 1:One population,one mean');
    writeln('Test 2:Means equal, standard deviations equal');
    writeln('Test 3:Means equal, standard deviations unequal');
    writeln;
    writeln('Choose hypothesis');
    repeat
      write('Enter 1, 2 or 3 : ')
    until ReadInt(hypothesis,1,3);

    writeln;
    case hypothesis of

      1:FirstHypothesis;
      2:SecondHypothesis;
      3:ThirdHypothesis
    end; { case }

    writeln;
    writeln('t-value = ',abs(tstat));
    writeln(df,' degrees of freedom');
end; { menu }

begin { main }
    writeln;
    writeln('Student''s t-Distribution Test');
    repeat
      writeln;
      menu;
      writeln;
    until NotAgain
end.
```

59

F-distribution

This program calculates percentile values and tail-end values for given values on an F-distribution curve. You must provide the value of F, the degrees of freedom in the numerator, and the degrees of freedom in the denominator.

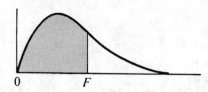

The F-distribution

The shaded region represents the percentile.

The F-distribution function is approximated using the following formula:

$$\text{percentile} = 1 - \frac{1}{2}(1 + a_1 y + a_2 y^2 + a_3 y^3 + a_4 y^4)^{-4} + \epsilon(y)$$

where: $a_1 = 0.196854$
$a_2 = 0.115194$
$a_3 = 0.000344$
$a_4 = 0.019527$

$$y = \left(F^{1/3}\left(1 - \frac{2}{9d_2}\right) - \left(1 - \frac{2}{9d_1}\right)\right)\left(\frac{2}{9d_1} + F^{2/3} \cdot \frac{2}{9d_2}\right)^{-1/2}$$

d_1 = degrees of freedom in numerator
d_2 = degrees of freedom in denominator

$$|\epsilon(y)| < 2.5 \cdot 10^{-4}$$

Examples:

What is the percentile and tail-end value on an F-distribution curve when the F-value is .474 and the degrees of freedom are 1 and 18?

What is the percentile and tail-end value when the F-value is 23.7 and the degrees of freedom are 3 and 6?

Run:

```
F-distribution

F-value: .474
Degrees of freedom in numerator: 1
Degrees of freedom in denominator: 18

Percentile =  4.93663E-1
Tail-end value =  5.06337E-1

Would you like another run? (y/n) y
```

```
F-value: 23.7
Degrees of freedom in numerator: 3
Degrees of freedom in denominator: 6

Percentile =  9.98358E-1
Tail-end value =  1.64180E-3

Would you like another run? (y/n) n
```

Program Listing:

```
program FDistribution(input,output);
uses transcend; { omit if not using Apple Pascal }
var
    Fvalue,
    percentile,
    tailend:real;
    numfree,
    denomfree:integer;

{$I ReadInt }
{$I ReadReal }
{$I RealRaise }
{$I IntRaise }
{$I NotAgain }


procedure ReadData;

begin
    repeat
      write('F-value: ' );
    until ReadReal(Fvalue);
    repeat
      write('Degrees of freedom in numerator: ');
    until ReadInt(numfree,1,maxint);
    repeat
      write('Degrees of freedom in denominator: ');
    until ReadInt(denomfree,1,maxint);
end;


procedure Calculate;

const
    a1 = 0.196854;
    a2 = 0.115194;
    a3 = 0.000344;
    a4 = 0.019527;

var
    temp : integer;
    ytemp,x,
    factor1,factor2:real;
    LessThanZero:boolean;

begin
    LessThanZero:= false;
    if abs(Fvalue) <1.0 then
      begin
```

163

```pascal
        Fvalue:=1/Fvalue;
        temp:= numfree;
        numfree:= denomfree;
        denomfree:= temp;
        LessThanZero:= true
      end;
    factor1:=2/(9*numfree);
    factor2:=2/(9*denomfree);

    ytemp:=abs(RealRaise(Fvalue,0.33333)*(1-factor2)-1+factor1) /
                sqrt((factor1+RealRaise(Fvalue ,0.666667)*factor2));

    if denomfree < 4 then
      ytemp:= ytemp * (1 + 0.08 * IntRaise(ytemp,4) /
                                      IntRaise(denomfree,3));

    x:= 0.5 / IntRaise((1 + ytemp * (a1 + ytemp * (a2 + ytemp *
                                      (a3 + ytemp * a4)))),4);

    if LessThanZero then
      x:= 1 - x;
    percentile:= 1 - x;
    tailend:= x;
    writeln;
    writeln('Percentile = ',percentile);
    writeln('Tail-end value = ',tailend)
end; { calculate }

begin { main }
    writeln;
    writeln('F-distribution');
    repeat
      writeln;
      ReadData;
      Calculate;
      writeln
    until NotAgain
end.
```

60
Linear Correlation Coefficient

This program computes the coefficient of correlation between two variables that have a linear relationship. You must enter the coordinates of a group of data points forming the regression line.

Example:

The height of twelve men and their sons is recorded in the table below. What is the coefficient of correlation between the heights of fathers and the heights of their sons?

Father	65	63	67	64	68	62	70	66	68	67	69	71
Son	68	66	68	65	69	66	68	65	71	67	68	70

Height in Inches

Run:

```
Linear Correlation Coefficient

Number of points: 12
Coordinates of point 1:    X: 65
                           Y: 68
Coordinates of point 2:    X: 63
                           Y: 66
Coordinates of point 3:    X: 67
                           Y: 68
Coordinates of point 4:    X: 64
                           Y: 65
Coordinates of point 5:    X: 68
                           Y: 69
Coordinates of point 6:    X: 62
                           Y: 66
Coordinates of point 7:    X: 70
                           Y: 68
Coordinates of point 8:    X: 66
                           Y: 65
Coordinates of point 9:    X: 68
                           Y: 71
Coordinates of point 10:   X: 67
                           Y: 67
Coordinates of point 11:   X: 69
                           Y: 68
Coordinates of point 12:   X: 71
                           Y: 70


Coefficient of correlation =  0.702652

Would you like another run? (y/n) n
```

Program Listing:

```
program LinCorrCoefficient(input,output);
uses transcend;   { omit if not using Apple Pascal }

var   NumPoints:integer;
      Coefficient, XCoor, YCoor, SumX, SumY,
      SumXSqr, SumYSqr, SumXtimesY : real;

{$I ReadInt }
{$I ReadReal }
{$I NotAgain }


function GetCoeff : real;
var   i:integer;
      GoAhead : boolean;

begin
  GoAhead:= false;
  repeat
    writeln;
    repeat
      write('Number of points: ')
    until ReadInt(NumPoints,2,maxint);
    SumX:= 0;
    SumY:= 0;
    SumXSqr:= 0;
    SumYSqr:= 0;
    SumXtimesY:= 0;
    for i:=1 to NumPoints do
      begin
        write('Coordinates of point ',i,':   ');
        repeat
          write('X: ')
        until ReadReal(XCoor);
        write(' ':25);
        if i>=10 then write(' ');
        repeat
          write('Y: ')
        until ReadReal(YCoor);
        SumX:= SumX + XCoor;
        SumY:= SumY + YCoor;
        SumXSqr:= SumXSqr + XCoor * XCoor;
        SumYSqr:= SumYSqr + YCoor * YCoor;
        SumXtimesY:= SumXtimesY + XCoor * YCoor;
      end;
    if (SumX*SumX = NumPoints*SumXSqr) or
                 (NumPoints*SumYSqr = SumY*SumY) then
      writeln('Coefficient of correlation cannot be calculated')
    else   GoAhead:= true
  until GoAhead;
  GetCoeff:= (NumPoints * SumXtimesY - SumX * SumY) /
             sqrt((NumPoints * SumXSqr - SumX * SumX) *
             (NumPoints * SumYSqr - SumY * SumY));
end; { function GetCoeff }


begin  { main }
  writeln;writeln('Linear Correlation Coefficient');
  writeln;
```

```
  repeat
    Coefficient:= GetCoeff;
    writeln;writeln;
    writeln('Coefficient of correlation = ',Coefficient:0:6);
    writeln
  until NotAgain
end.
```

61
Linear Regression

This program fits a straight line to pairs of coordinates using the method of least squares. The program prints the equation of the line, the coefficient of determination, the coefficient of correlation, and the standard error of estimate. Once the line has been fitted, you can predict values of y for given values of x.

Example:

The table below shows the height and weight of 11 male college students. Fit a curve to these points. How much would the average 70 inch and 72 inch male student weigh?

Height (inches)	71	73	64	65	61	70	65	72	63	67	64
Weight (pounds)	160	183	154	168	159	180	145	210	132	168	141

Run:

```
Linear Regression

Number of points: 11
Coordinates of point 1:    X: 71
                           Y: 160
Coordinates of point 2:    X: 73
                           Y: 183
Coordinates of point 3:    X: 64
                           Y: 154
Coordinates of point 4:    X: 65
                           Y: 168
Coordinates of point 5:    X: 61
                           Y: 159
Coordinates of point 6:    X: 70
                           Y: 180
Coordinates of point 7:    X: 65
                           Y: 145
Coordinates of point 8:    X: 72
                           Y: 210
Coordinates of point 9:    X: 63
                           Y: 132
Coordinates of point 10:   X: 67
                           Y: 168
Coordinates of point 11:   X: 64
                           Y: 141

F(x)= -106.792     + ( 4.04722 * X )

Coefficient of determination (R-squared) =   0.55626
Coefficient of correlation =   0.74583
Standard error of estimate =   15.4134


Interpolation:   (Enter 0 to end program)
```

```
x= 70
y= 176.514

x= 72
y= 184.608

x= 0
```

Program Listing:

```pascal
program LinearRegression(input,output);
uses transcend;   { omit if not using Apple Pascal }

var   NumPoints:integer;
      XCoor, YCoor, SumX, SumY, CoeffOfDet, StandErrNumerator,
      SumXSqr, SumYSqr, SumXtimesY, A, B: real;

{$I ReadInt }
{$I ReadReal }

procedure GetData;
var  i:integer;

begin
  repeat
    write('Number of points: ')
  until ReadInt(NumPoints,1,maxint);
  SumX:= 0;
  SumY:= 0;
  SumXSqr:= 0;
  SumYSqr:= 0;
  SumXtimesY:= 0;
  for i:=1 to NumPoints do
    begin
      write('Coordinates of point ',i:0,':   ');
      repeat
        write('X: ')
      until ReadReal(XCoor);
      write(' ':25);
      repeat
        write('Y: ')
      until ReadReal(YCoor);
      SumX:= SumX + XCoor;
      SumY:= SumY + YCoor;
      SumXSqr:= SumXSqr + XCoor * XCoor;
      SumYSqr:= SumYSqr + YCoor * YCoor;
      SumXtimesY:= SumXtimesY + XCoor * YCoor;
    end;
  B:= (NumPoints*SumXtimesY - SumY*SumX)
      / (NumPoints*SumXSqr - SumX*SumX);
  A:= (SumY - B*SumX) / NumPoints;
end; { procedure GetData }

procedure CompRegressAnalysis;
var  temp:real;

begin
  temp:= B * (SumXtimesY - SumX * SumY / NumPoints);
  CoeffOfDet:= temp / (SumYSqr - SumY*SumY/NumPoints);
  StandErrNumerator:=SumYSqr - SumY * SumY / NumPoints - temp;
```

```
    writeln;
    writeln('Coefficient of determination (R-squared) = ',CoeffOfDet);
    writeln('Coefficient of correlation = ',sqrt(abs(CoeffOfDet)));
    writeln('Standard error of estimate = ',
                          sqrt(StandErrNumerator/(NumPoints - 2)));
end; { procedure CompRegressAnalysis }

procedure Interpolate;
var x:real;

begin
    writeln('Interpolation:   (Enter 0 to end program)');
    repeat
      writeln;
      repeat
        write('x= ')
      until ReadReal(x);
      if x<>0 then
        writeln('y=',A + B * x);
    until x=0;
end; { procedure Interpolate }


begin   { main }
    writeln;writeln('Linear Regression');
    writeln;
    GetData;
    writeln;writeln('F(x)= ',A,' + (',B,' * X )');
    CompRegressAnalysis;
    writeln;writeln;
    Interpolate;
end.
```

62
Multiple Linear Regression

This program finds the coefficients of a multiple variable linear equation using the method of least squares. The equation is the following form:

$$y = c + a_1 x_1 + a_2 x_2 + \ldots a_n x_n$$

where: y = dependent variable
c = constant
$a_1, a_2, \ldots, a_n$ = coefficients of independent variables $x_1, x_2, \ldots, x_n$

The constant and the coefficients are printed.

You must provide the x and y coordinates of known data points. Once the equation has been found using the data you enter, you may predict values of the dependent variables for given values of the independent variables.

Program Notes

You can adjust the maximum number of known points, now set at 8. The constant ArrayLimit must equal no more than the maximum plus one (1), and the constant SArrayLimit must equal two (2) more than the maximum. For example, for a maximum of 6 points, set ArrayLimit equal to 7 and SArrayLimit to 8.

Example:

The table below shows the age, height, and weight of eight boys. Using weight as the dependent variable, fit a curve to the data. Estimate the weight of a seven-year-old boy who is 51 inches tall.

Age	8	9	6	10	8	9	9	7
Height	48	49	44	59	55	51	55	50
Weight	59	55	50	80	61	75	67	58

Run:

```
Multiple Linear Regression

Number of known points: 8
Number of independent variables: 2
Point 1
   Variable 1: 8
   Variable 2: 48
   Dependent variable: 59
Point 2
   Variable 1: 9
   Variable 2: 49
   Dependent variable: 55
Point 3
   Variable 1: 6
   Variable 2: 44
   Dependent variable: 50
```

```
Point 4
  Variable 1: 10
  Variable 2: 59
  Dependent variable: 80
Point 5
  Variable 1: 8
  Variable 2: 55
  Dependent variable: 61
Point 6
  Variable 1: 9
  Variable 2: 51
  Dependent variable: 75
Point 7
  Variable 1: 9
  Variable 2: 55
  Dependent variable: 67
Point 8
  Variable 1: 7
  Variable 2: 50
  Dependent variable: 58

Equation Coefficients:
      Constant:-1.57021E1
Variable( 1 ): 3.68085
Variable( 2 ): 9.43262E-1

Coefficient of determination, (R - squared) =  7.15697E-1
Coefficient of multiple correlation =  8.45989E-1
Standard error of estimate =  6.42888

Interpolation:   (enter 0 to end)
Variable 1: 7
Variable 2: 51
Dependent variable =  5.81702E1

Variable 1: 0

Would you like another run? (y/n) n
```

Program Listing:

```pascal
program MultipleLinearRegression(input,output);
uses transcend;  { omit if not using Apple Pascal }

const   ArrayLimit = 9;   { maximum known points is 8 }
        SArrayLimit = 10;

type  LinearArray=array[1..ArrayLimit] of real;
      SquareArray=array[1..ArrayLimit,1..SArrayLimit] of real;

var   equations : SquareArray;
      IndepVars,S,T : LinearArray;
      NumPoints, NumVariables: integer;
      Z, m, CoeffOfDet, StandardError : real;

{$I ReadInt }
{$I ReadReal }
procedure Initialize;

var   i,j:integer;
```

```
begin
  for i:=1 to ArrayLimit do
    begin
      IndepVars[i]:=0;
      S[i]:=0;
      T[i]:=0
    end;
  for i:=1 to ArrayLimit do
    for j:=1 to SArrayLimit do
      equations[i,j]:=0;
end; { procedure Initialize }



procedure InputData;
var  i,j,k,m : integer;

begin
  repeat
    write('Number of known points: ')
  until ReadInt(NumPoints,1,ArrayLimit-1);
  repeat
    write('Number of independent variables: ')
  until ReadInt(NumVariables,1,ArrayLimit-1);
  IndepVars[1]:=1;
  for i:=1 to NumPoints do
    begin
      writeln('Point ',i:0);
      for j:=1 to NumVariables do
        repeat
          write('  Variable ',j:0,': ')
        until ReadReal(IndepVars[j+1]);
      repeat
        write('  Dependent variable: ')
      until ReadReal(IndepVars[NumVariables+2]);
      for k:=1 to NumVariables+1 do
        for m:=1 to NumVariables+2 do
          begin
            equations[k,m]:=equations[k,m]
                              + IndepVars[k]*IndepVars[m];
            S[k]:= equations[k,NumVariables+2];
          end;
      S[NumVariables+2]:=S[NumVariables+2]
                          + IndepVars[NumVariables+2] *
                                IndepVars[NumVariables+2];

    end; { for i }
end; { procedure InputData }

function SolveEquations : boolean;
var  i,j,k,m : integer;
     hold, P, R : real;
     NoSolution : boolean;

begin
  for i:=2 to NumVariables+1 do
    T[i]:= equations[1,i];
  for i:=1 to NumVariables + 1 do
    begin
      j:=i-1;
```

```pascal
      NoSolution:= true;
      while (j<NumVariables+1) and NoSolution do
        begin
          j:=j+1;
          NoSolution:= equations[j,i]=0
        end;
      if NoSolution then
        begin
          writeln('No unique solution');
          i:=NumVariables+1
        end
      else
        begin
          for k:=1 to NumVariables+2 do
            begin
              hold:= equations[i,k];
              equations[i,k]:=equations[j,k];
              equations[j,k]:=hold
            end;
          Z:=1/equations[i,i];
          for k:=1 to NumVariables+2 do
            equations[i,k]:=Z*equations[i,k];
          for j:=1 to NumVariables+1 do
            if j<>i then
              begin
                Z:= -equations[j,i];
                for k:=1 to NumVariables+2 do
                  equations[j,k]:=equations[j,k]+Z*equations[i,k];
              end;
        end;
    end; { for i loop }
  if not NoSolution then
    begin
      P:= 0;
      for j:=2 to NumVariables+1 do
        P:= P + equations[j, NumVariables+2] * (S[j] - T[j] *
                                                S[1] / NumPoints);
      R:= S[NumVariables+2] - S[1] * S[1] / NumPoints;
      StandardError:= (R - P) / (NumPoints - NumVariables - 1);
      CoeffOfDet:= P / R;
    end;
  SolveEquations :=not NoSolution
end; { function SolveEquations }


procedure PrintResults;
var  i:integer;

begin
  writeln('Equation Coefficients:');
  writeln('      Constant:',equations[1,NumVariables+2]);
  for i:=2 to NumVariables+1 do
    writeln('Variable( ',i-1:0,' ):',equations[i,NumVariables+2]);
  writeln;
  writeln('Coefficient of determination (R - squared) = ',
                                              CoeffOfDet);
  writeln('Coefficient of multiple correlation = ',
                                    sqrt(abs(CoeffOfDet)));
  writeln('Standard error of estimate = ',sqrt(abs(StandardError)));
  writeln;
end; { procedure printresults }
```

```
procedure interpolate;
var  p, x : real;
     j : integer;

begin
  write('Interpolation:   (enter 0 to end program)');
  repeat
    writeln;
    p:=equations[1,NumVariables+2];
    for j:=1 to NumVariables do
      begin
        repeat
          write('Variable ',j:0,' ');
        until ReadReal(x);
        if x<>0 then
          p:=p+equations[j+1,NumVariables+2] * x
        else
          j:=NumVariables;
      end;
    if x<>0 then
      writeln('Dependent variable = ',p);
  until x=0;
end; { procedure interpolate }


begin  { main }
  writeln; writeln('Multiple Linear Regression');
  writeln;
  Initialize;
  InputData;
  if SolveEquations then
    begin
      writeln;
      PrintResults;
      Interpolate
    end;
end.
```

63
*N*th Order Regression

This program finds the coefficients of an *N*th order equation using the method of least squares. The equation is the following form:

$$y = c + a_1x + a_2x^2 + \ldots a_nx^n$$

where: y = dependent variable
c = constant
$a_1, a_2, \ldots, a_n$ = coefficients of independent variables $x, x^2, \ldots, x^n$

The equation coefficients, coefficient of determination, and standard error of estimate are printed.

You must provide the x and y coordinates for known data points. Once the equation has been computed, you may predict values of y for given values of x.

Program Notes

The constants "DegreePlus1," "DegPlus 2," and "TwoDegPlus1" depend on the degree of the equation:

DegreePlus1 = D + 1
DegPlus2   = D + 2
TwoDegPlus1 = 2D + 1

where D is the degree of the equation. For example, if D = 2, then DegreePlus1 = 3, DegPlus2 = 4, and TwoDegPlus1 = 5.

Example:

The table below gives the stopping distance (reaction plus braking distance) of an automobile at various speeds. Fit an exponential curve to the data. Estimate the stopping distance at 90 m.p.h.

M.P.H.	20	30	40	50	60	70
Stopping distance	54	90	138	206	292	396

Run:

```
Nth Order Regression

Degree of equation: 2
Number of known points: 6
Coordinates of point 1:
          X: 20
          Y: 54
Coordinates of point 2:
          X: 30
          Y: 90
Coordinates of point 3:
          X: 40
          Y: 138
```

```
Coordinates of point 4:
              X: 50
              Y: 206
Coordinates of point 5:
              X: 60
              Y: 292
Coordinates of point 6:
              X: 70
              Y: 396


Constant =  41.7720
1 degree coefficient = -1.09574
2 degree coefficient =  0.08786

Coefficient of determination (R squared) =  0.99993
Coefficient of correlation =  0.99996
Standard error of estimate =  1.41973


Interpolation:  (Enter 0 to end program)

X = 90
Y =   654.801

X = 0
```

Program Listing:

```pascal
program NthOrderRegression(input,output);
uses transcend;   { Omit if not using Apple Pascal }

const   DegreePlus1 = 7;  { = D+1 } { where D is the maximum }
        DegPlus2    = 8;  { = D+2 } { degree of the equation }
        TwoDegPlus1 = 13; { = 2D+1 }

type    LinearArray = array[1..DegreePlus1] of real;
        DoubleArray = array[1..TwoDegPlus1] of real;
        SquareArray = array[1..DegreePlus1 , 1..DegPlus2] of real;

var  A : DoubleArray;
     R : SquareArray;
     T : LinearArray;
     NumPoints, degree : integer;
     CoeffOfDet, StandardError : real;

{$I ReadInt }
{$I ReadReal }
{$I IntRaise }

procedure Initialize;
var  j, k : integer;

begin
   for j:=1 to DegreePlus1 do
     begin
       T[j]:= 0;
       A[j]:= 0;
       A[DegreePlus1 + j - 1]:= 0;
     end;
   for j:=1 to DegreePlus1 do
```

```
      for k:=1 to DegPlus2 do
        R[j,k]:= 0;
end;  { procedure Initialize }


procedure InputData;
var  h, j, k : integer;
     x, y : real;

begin
  repeat
    write('Degree of equation: ')
  until ReadInt(degree, 1, DegreePlus1 - 1);
  repeat
    write('Number of known points: ')
  until ReadInt(NumPoints, 1, maxint);
  A[1]:= NumPoints;
  for h:=1 to NumPoints do
    begin
      writeln('Coordinates of point ',h:0,': ');
      repeat
        write('X':15,': ')
      until ReadReal(x);
      repeat
        write('Y':15,': ')
      until ReadReal(y);
      for j:=2 to 2*degree+1 do
        A[j]:=A[j] + IntRaise(x,j-1);
      for k:=1 to degree + 1 do
        begin
          R[k, degree + 2]:= T[k] + y * IntRaise(x, k-1);
          T[k]:= R[k, degree + 2]
        end;
    T[degree + 2]:= T[degree + 2] + y*y;
  end;
end;  { procedure InputData }


function SolveEquations : boolean;
var  h, j, k : integer;
     hold, p, q, z : real;
     NoSolution : boolean;

begin
  for j:=1 to degree + 1 do
    for k:=1 to degree + 1 do
      R[j,k]:= A[j + k -1];
  for j:=1 to degree + 1 do
    begin
      k:= j - 1;
      NoSolution:= true;
      while (k<degree + 1) and NoSolution do
        begin
          k:= k + 1;
          NoSolution:= R[k,j] = 0
        end;
      if NoSolution then
        begin
          writeln('No unique solution');
          j:= degree + 1
        end
```

```
        else
          begin
            for h:=1 to degree + 2 do
              begin
                hold:= R[j,h];
                R[j,h]:= R[k,h];
                R[k,h]:= hold
              end;
            z:= 1 / R[j,j];
            for h:=1 to degree + 2 do
              R[j,h]:= z * R[j,h];
            for k:=1 to degree + 1 do
              if k<>j then
                begin
                  z:= -R[k,j];
                  for h:=1 to degree + 2 do
                    R[k,h]:= R[k,h] + z * R[j,h]
                end;
          end;
      end;
  if not NoSolution then
    begin
      p:= 0;
      for j:=2 to degree + 1 do
        p:= p + R[j,degree + 2] * (T[j] - A[j] * T[1] / NumPoints);
      q:= T[degree + 2] - T[1] * T[1] / NumPoints;
      CoeffOfDet:= p / q;
      StandardError:= (q - p) / (NumPoints - degree - 1);
    end;
  SolveEquations:= not NoSolution;
end;  { function SolveEquations }

procedure PrintResults;
var  j : integer;

begin
  writeln('Constant = ', R[1,degree + 2]);
  for j:=1 to degree do
    writeln(j:0,' degree coefficient = ',R[j + 1 , degree + 2]);
  writeln;
  writeln('Coefficient of determination (R squared) = ',
                                        CoeffOfDet);
  writeln('Coefficient of correlation = ', sqrt(abs(CoeffOfDet)));
  writeln('Standard error of estimate = ',
                               sqrt(abs(StandardError)));
end; { procedure PrintResults }

procedure Interpolate;
var  j : integer;
     x, p : real;

begin
  writeln('Interpolation:   (Enter 0 to end program)');
  repeat
    writeln;
    p:= R[1,degree + 2];
    repeat
      write('X = ');
    until ReadReal(x);
    if x<>0 then
```

```
      begin
        for j:=1 to degree do
          p:= p + R[j + 1 , degree + 2] * IntRaise(x , j);
          writeln('Y = ', p)
      end;
  until x = 0;
end;  { procedure Interpolate }

begin  { main }
  writeln; writeln('Nth Order Regression');
  writeln;
  Initialize;
  InputData;
  if SolveEquations then
    begin
      writeln;
      PrintResults;
      writeln;writeln;
      Interpolate
    end;
end.
```

64
Geometric Regression

This program fits a geometric curve to a set of coordinates by the method of least squares and prints the equation of the curve, the coefficient of determination, coefficient of correlation, and standard error of estimate. You must provide the x and y coordinates of known data points. Once the curve has been fitted, you can predict values of y for given values of x.

Example:

An experiment measures gas pressures at various volumes. The relationship between pressure and volume is:

$$PV^K = C$$

where: P = pressure
V = volume
C and K are constants

This formula can be rewritten in standard geometric form:

$$P = CV^{-K}$$

Fit a geometric curve to the following data and estimate the pressure of 90.0 cubic inches of the gas.

Volume	56.1	60.7	73.2	88.3	120.1	187.5
Pressure	57.0	51.0	39.2	30.2	19.6	10.5

Run:

```
Geometric Regression

Number of points: 6
Coordinates of point 1:    X: 56.1
                           Y: 57
Coordinates of point 2:    X: 60.7
                           Y: 51
Coordinates of point 3:    X: 73.2
                           Y: 39.2
Coordinates of point 4:    X: 88.3
                           Y: 30.2
Coordinates of point 5:    X: 120.1
                           Y: 19.6
Coordinates of point 6:    X: 187.5
                           Y: 10.5

F(x) =   16103.4      * X to the -1.40155  power

Coefficient of determination (R-squared) =   1.00000
Coeffficient of correlation =   1.00000
Standard error of estimate =   0.001505
```

```
Interpolation:   (Enter 0 to end)

x= 90
y= 29.3735

x= 0

Would you like another run? (y/n) n
```

Program Listing:

```pascal
program GeometricRegression(input,output);
uses transcend;   { omit if not using Apple Pascal }

var   NumPoints:integer;
      XCoor, YCoor, SumLogX, SumLogY, CoeffOfDet, StandErrNumerator,
      SumXSqr, SumYSqr, SumXtimesY, A, B: real;

{$I ReadInt }
{$I ReadReal }
{$I RealRaise }
{$I NotAgain }


procedure GetData;
var  i : integer;
     GoAhead : boolean;

begin
  GoAhead:= false;
  repeat
    writeln;
    repeat
      write('Number of points: ')
    until ReadInt(NumPoints,2,maxint);
    SumLogX:= 0;
    SumLogY:= 0;
    SumXSqr:= 0;
    SumYSqr:= 0;
    SumXtimesY:= 0;
    for i:=1 to NumPoints do
      begin
        write('Coordinates of point ',i,':  ');
        repeat
          write('X: ')
        until ReadReal(XCoor) and (XCoor > 0);
        write(' ':25);
        if i>=10 then write(' ');
        repeat
          write('Y: ')
        until ReadReal(YCoor) and (YCoor > 0);
        XCoor:= ln(XCoor);
        YCoor:= ln(YCoor);
        SumLogX:= SumLogX + XCoor;
        SumLogY:= SumLogY + YCoor;
        SumXSqr:= SumXSqr + XCoor * XCoor;
        SumYSqr:= SumYSqr + YCoor * YCoor;
        SumXtimesY:= SumXtimesY + XCoor * YCoor;
      end;
    if NumPoints * SumXSqr = SumLogX * SumLogX then
      writeln('Regression cannot be calculated')
```

```
      else  GoAhead:= true
    until GoAhead;
   B:= (NumPoints*SumXtimesY - SumLogY*SumLogX)
       / (NumPoints*SumXSqr - SumLogX*SumLogX);
   A:= (SumLogY - B*SumLogX) / NumPoints;
end; { procedure GetData }


procedure CompRegressAnalysis;
var  temp:real;

begin
   temp:= B * (SumXtimesY - SumLogX * SumLogY / NumPoints);
   CoeffOfDet:= abs(temp / (SumYSqr - SumLogY*SumLogY/NumPoints));
   StandErrNumerator:=SumYSqr - SumLogY * SumLogY / NumPoints - temp;
   writeln;
   writeln('Coefficient of determination (R-squared) = ',CoeffOfDet);
   writeln('Coeffficient of correlation = ',sqrt(abs(CoeffOfDet)));
   if NumPoints = 2 then NumPoints:=3;
   writeln('Standard error of estimate = ',
                      sqrt(abs(StandErrNumerator/(NumPoints - 2))));
end; { procedure CompRegressAnalysis }


procedure Interpolate;
var x:real;

begin
   writeln('Interpolation:   (Enter 0 to end)');
   repeat
     writeln;
     repeat
       write('x= ')
     until ReadReal(x);
     if x<>0 then
       writeln('y=',exp(A)* RealRaise(x,B));
   until x=0;
end; { procedure Interpolate }



begin   { main }
   writeln;writeln('Geometric Regression');
   writeln;
   repeat
     GetData;
     writeln;writeln('F(x) = ',exp(A),' * X to the ',B,' power');
     CompRegressAnalysis;
     writeln;writeln;
     Interpolate;
     writeln
   until NotAgain
end.
```

65
Exponential Regression

This program calculates the coefficients of an equation for an exponential curve and prints the equation's coefficients, the coefficient of determination, coefficient of correlation, and standard error of estimate. The equation is in the form:

$$f(x) = ae^{bx}$$

where a and b are the calculated coefficients

You must provide the x and y coordinates for the known data points. Once the curve has been fitted, you may predict values of y for given values of x.

Example:

The table below shows the bacteria count in a culture, with measurement at hourly intervals. Fit an exponential curve to the data and estimate the bacteria count at seven hours.

Number of Hours	0	1	2	3	4	5	6
Number of Bacteria	25	38	58	89	135	206	315

Run:

```
Exponential Regression

Number of points: 7
Coordinates of point 1:    X: 0
                           Y: 25
Coordinates of point 2:    X: 1
                           Y: 38
Coordinates of point 3:    X: 2
                           Y: 58
Coordinates of point 4:    X: 3
                           Y: 89
Coordinates of point 5:    X: 4
                           Y: 135
Coordinates of point 6:    X: 5
                           Y: 206
Coordinates of point 7:    X: 6
                           Y: 315

A =   24.9617
B =   0.422375

Coefficient of determination (R-squared) = 0.999989
Coefficient of correlation = 0.999995
Standard error of estimate = 0.003283


Interpolation:   (enter 0 to end)
```

x= 7
y= 480.086

x= 0

Would you like another run? (y/n) n

Program Listing:

```pascal
program ExponentialRegression(input,output);
uses transcend;  { omit if not using Apple Pascal }

var  NumPoints : integer;
     XCoor, YCoor, SumX, SumLogY, CoeffOfDet, StandErrNumerator,
     SumXSqr, SumYSqr, SumXtimesY, A, B: real;

{$I ReadInt }
{$I ReadReal }
{$I NotAgain }


procedure GetData;
var  i : integer;
     GoAhead : boolean;

begin
  GoAhead:= false;
  repeat
    writeln;
    repeat
      write('Number of points: ')
    until ReadInt(NumPoints,2,maxint);
    SumX:= 0;
    SumLogY:= 0;
    SumXSqr:= 0;
    SumYSqr:= 0;
    SumXtimesY:= 0;
    for i:=1 to NumPoints do
      begin
        write('Coordinates of point ',i,':   ');
        repeat
          write('X: ')
        until ReadReal(XCoor);
        write(' ':25);
        if i>=10 then write(' ');
        repeat
          write('Y: ')
        until ReadReal(YCoor) and (YCoor > 0);
        YCoor:= ln(YCoor);
        SumX:= SumX + XCoor;
        SumLogY:= SumLogY + YCoor;
        SumXSqr:= SumXSqr + XCoor * XCoor;
        SumYSqr:= SumYSqr + YCoor * YCoor;
        SumXtimesY:= SumXtimesY + XCoor * YCoor;
      end;
    if NumPoints*SumXSqr = SumX*SumX then
      writeln('Regression cannot be calculated')
    else  GoAhead:= true
  until  GoAhead;
  B:= (NumPoints*SumXtimesY - SumLogY*SumX)
      / (NumPoints*SumXSqr - SumX*SumX);
```

```
    A:= (SumLogY - B*SumX) / NumPoints;
end; { procedure GetData }

procedure CompRegressAnalysis;
var  temp:real;

begin
   temp:= B * (SumXtimesY - SumX * SumLogY / NumPoints);
   CoeffOfDet:= abs(temp / (SumYSqr - SumLogY*SumLogY/NumPoints));
   StandErrNumerator:=SumYSqr - SumLogY * SumLogY / NumPoints - temp;
   writeln;
   writeln('Coefficient of determination (R-squared) =',CoeffOfDet:0:6);
   writeln('Coefficient of correlation =',sqrt(abs(CoeffOfDet)):0:6);
   if NumPoints=2 then NumPoints:=3;
   writeln('Standard error of estimate =',
                            sqrt(abs(StandErrNumerator/(NumPoints - 2))):0:6);
end;  { procedure CompRegressAnalysis }


procedure Interpolate;
var x:real;

begin
   writeln('Interpolation:   (enter 0 to end)');
   repeat
     writeln;
     repeat
       write('x= ')
     until ReadReal(x);
     if x<>0 then
       writeln('y= ',(exp(A) * exp(B*x)):0:6);
   until x=0;
end;  { procedure Interpolate }


begin  { main }
   writeln;writeln('Exponential Regression');
   writeln;
   repeat
     GetData;
     writeln;writeln('A = ',exp(A):0:6);
     writeln('B = ',B:0:6);
     CompRegressAnalysis;
     writeln;writeln;
     Interpolate;
     writeln
   until NotAgain
end.
```

66
System Reliability

This program calculates the reliability of an operating system that is subject to wearout and chance failure. You must enter the system's operating time and the wearout time and failure rate of each component.

Example:

Compute the reliability of a computer system operating for 1000 hours with the components shown in the list below:

	Wearout (hours)	Failure
CPU	15,000	0.00020
Terminal	3,000	0.00010
Disk	3,000	0.00015
Printer	1,500	0.00015

Run:

```
System Reliability

Operating time in hours? 1000
Number of components: 4

Component 1
   Average wearout time= 15000
   Average failure rate= .0002
Component 2
   Average wearout time= 3000
   Average failure rate= .0001
Component 3
   Average wearout time= 3000
   Average failure rate= .00015
Component 4
   Average wearout time= 1500
   Average failure rate= .00015

System reliability =   0.135335

Would you like another run? (y/n) n
```

Program Listing:

```
program SystemReliability(input,output);
uses transcend;  { omit if not using Apple Pascal }
const  LowExpBound = -87.3365;

var  NumOfComponents:integer;
     reliability, time, WearOut, failure, sum:real;


{$I ReadInt }
{$I ReadReal }
{$I NotAgain }

function GetData:real;

var  i:integer;
     GoAhead : boolean;

begin
  repeat
    GoAhead:= true;
    sum:= 0;
    repeat
      write('Operating time in hours? ')
    until ReadReal(time) and (time>0);
    repeat
      write('Number of components: ')
    until ReadInt(NumOfComponents,1,maxint);
    writeln;
    for i:=1 to NumOfComponents do
      begin
        writeln('Component ',i);
        repeat
          write('  Average wearout time= ')
        until ReadReal(wearout) and (wearout > 0);
        repeat
          write('  Average failure rate= ')
        until ReadReal(failure) and (failure > 0) and (failure <= 1);
        sum:=sum + 1/wearout + failure
      end;
    if -sum*time <= LowExpBound then
      begin
        writeln('Your system reliability is less than ');
        writeln(exp(LowExpBound),' and cannot be calculated');
        GoAhead:= false
      end
  until GoAhead;
  GetData:= exp(-sum * time);
end;  { function GetData }


begin  { main }
  writeln;writeln('System Reliability');
  writeln;
  repeat
    reliability:= GetData;
    writeln;writeln('System reliability = ',reliability:0:6);
    writeln;
  until NotAgain;
end.
```

67
Average Growth Rate, Future Projections

This program calculates an average growth rate from a series of figures representing past years, and then projects figures for future years. You provide the known figures for past years. In response to the prompt "What do your figures represent?" you may name sales, earnings, number of employees, clients, or any other aspect of a company. Your figures could also represent books, as in the example below.

Example:

The borrowing records of Coconino County Library are tabulated in the graph below. What is the average growth rate? How many books can it expect to lend in its tenth and twentieth years of service?

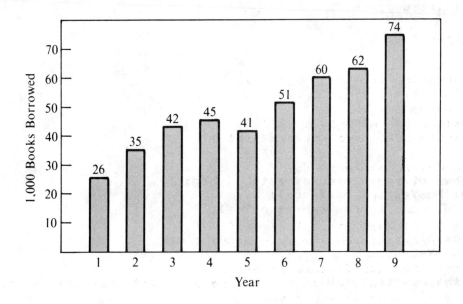

Run:

```
Average Growth Rate, Future Projections

Number of years figures established: 9
What do your figures represent? Books Borrowed
Figure: year 1: 26
        year 2: 35
        year 3: 42
        year 4: 45
        year 5: 41
        year 6: 51
        year 7: 60
        year 8: 62
        year 9: 74
Average growth rate =  11.8800   %

Enter 0 to end
projected Books Borrowed for year: 10
            = 81.2883
```

```
projected Books Borrowed for year: 20
                      = 249.874
projected Books Borrowed for year: 0

Would you like another run? (y/n) n
```

Program Listing:

```
program GrowthRate(input,output);
uses transcend;  { omit if not using Apple Pascal }

const MaxYears=20;

type  LinearAray=array[1..MaxYears] of real;

var  PastFigures:LinearArray;
     GrowFactor, GrowRate: real;
     Name : string[20];
     NumYears : integer;

{$I ReadReal }
{$I ReadInt }
{$I IntRaise }


procedure InputData;
var  j : integer;

begin
  repeat
    write('Number of years figures established: ')
  until ReadInt(NumYears,1,MaxYears);
  write('What do your figures represent? ');
  readln(Name);
  write('Figure: ');
  for j:=1 to NumYears do
    begin
      if j<>1 then write(' ':8);
      repeat
        write('year ',j:0,': ')
      until ReadReal(PastFigures[j]);
    end;
end;  { procedure InputData }

function AverageGrowthRate:real;
var  CurrentLog, SumLogs, SumFactoredLogs,
     LogGrowthRate : real;
     j : integer;
begin
  SumLogs:=ln(PastFigures[1]);
  SumFactoredLogs:=0;
  for j:=2 to NumYears do
    begin
      CurrentLog:= ln(PastFigures[j]);
      SumLogs:= SumLogs + CurrentLog;
      SumFactoredLogs:= SumFactoredLogs + (j-1) * CurrentLog;
    end;
  LogGrowthRate:= 6 * (2 * SumFactoredLogs
            / (NumYears - 1) - SumLogs)/ NumYears / (NumYears + 1);
  GrowRate:= exp(LogGrowthRate) - 1;
```

190

```
   GrowFactor:= exp(SumLogs / NumYears - LogGrowthRate
                   * (NumYears -1) / 2);
   AverageGrowthRate:=trunc(GrowRate * 10000 + 0.5) / 100;
end; { function CalcGrowthRate }

procedure ProjectFigures;
var  year : integer;
     ProjFigure : real;

begin
  writeln('Enter 0 to end program');
  repeat
    repeat
      write('projected ',Name,' for year: ')
    until ReadInt(year, 0, maxint);
    if year<>0 then
      begin
        ProjFigure:= GrowFactor * IntRaise(1 + GrowRate,year-1);
        writeln('=':27,trunc(ProjFigure*100 + 0.5) / 100);
      end;
  until year = 0;
end;  { procedure ProjectFigures }


begin  { main }
  writeln; writeln('Average Growth Rate, Future Projections');
  writeln;
  InputData;
  writeln('Average growth rate = ',AverageGrowthRate,' %');
  writeln;
  ProjectFigures;
end.
```

68
Federal Withholding Taxes

This program calculates the amount of federal income and FICA taxes withheld from one's earnings. You must provide employee information as to marital status, the number of exemptions claimed, the amount of taxable pay, and year-to-date taxable pay.

Program Notes

You can use this program for the common pay periods (for example, 52 times per year represents a weekly paycheck) or for less common pay periods, which ask for the number of work days in the working year. Within the body of the program, annualized pay is used for the calculations.

A great deal of tax information varies from year to year. This information is contained in easily modified constants and variables. To be sure that the tax information is up-to-date, consult IRS Circular E, Table 7, before running the program.

The arrays "MarBracket" and "SingBracket" contain the bounds of the tax brackets for married and single taxpayers. Notice that for purposes of withholding, the IRS lumps taxpayers into two groups: single and married. Thus, even heads of households who are single are withheld at the "single" rate.

The tax bases for married and single taxpayers are contained in the arrays "MarConst" and "SingConst," and the tax rates for married and single taxpayers in each tax bracket are contained in the arrays "MarRate" and "SingRate." The constant "MaxGroups" is one (1) more than the number of tax brackets. MaxGroups is set equal to 8 and should not need to be modified.

Within the procedure "conversion," the case statement calculates the exemption allowance for different pay periods and for the number of exemptions. Some of these numbers may change. For instance, with 52 pay periods per year (weekly), the quantity "19.23" is multiplied by the number of exemptions (the variable Nexempt) to yield a number which is subtracted from gross pay (the variable subtract). The variable "aberrant" is used with the miscellaneous pay periods and calculates a daily rate.

Examples:

Judy earns $900.00 per month. The payroll clerk is figuring her March paycheck. Judy is single and claims only herself as a dependent. What amounts are withheld from her paycheck?

Dr. Berger has earned $1,408.75 this month. So far this year she has grossed $20,188.72. She is married and claims four dependents. What amounts will be withheld this month for the federal government?

Run:

```
Federal Withholding Taxes

Current taxable pay: 900
Year-to-date taxable pay: 1800
Marital status: (S=single   M=married) s
Number of pay periods per year: 12
Number of withholding exemptions: 1
Federal income tax withheld:  1.39083E2
FICA tax =  5.05162E1
Would you like another run? (y/n) y

Current taxable pay: 1408.75
Year-to-date taxable pay: 20188.72
```

192

```
Marital status: (S=single   M=married) m
Number of pay periods per year: 12
Number of withholding exemptions: 4
Federal income tax withheld:  2.03993E2
FICA tax =  7.88577E1
Would you like another run? (y/n) n
```

Program Listing:

```
program FederalWithholding(input,output);
const
    MaxGroups = 8;
type
    TaxTable = array[1..MaxGroups] of real;
var
  YTDpay,
  income,
  remainder,
  subtract,
  AnnualTaxbl,
  tax:real;
  Nexempt,
  period:integer;
  MarBracket,MarConst,MarRate,
  SingBracket,SingConst,SingRate : TaxTable;

{$I ReadInt }
{$I ReadReal }
{$I NotAgain}

procedure initialize;
begin
  MarBracket[1]:= 2400.00;   (* tax brackets for married status *)
  MarBracket[2]:= 7650.00;
  MarBracket[3]:= 10900.00;
  MarBracket[4]:= 15400.00;
  MarBracket[5]:= 23250.00;
  MarBracket[6]:= 28900.00;
  MarBracket[7]:= 34200.00;
  MarBracket[8]:= 1E10;
  MarConst[1]:= 0.00; (* base tax for tax brackets (married) *)
  MarConst[2]:= 735.00;
  MarConst[3]:= 1255.00;
  MarConst[4]:= 2155.00;
  MarConst[5]:= 4117.60;
  MarConst[6]:= 5869.00;
  MarConst[7]:= 7671.00;
  MarRate[1]:= 0.14;   (* tax rates for married status *)
  MarRate[2]:= 0.16;
  MarRate[3]:= 0.20;
  MarRate[4]:= 0.25;
  MarRate[5]:= 0.31;
  MarRate[6]:= 0.34;
  MarRate[7]:= 0.37;
  SingBracket[1]:= 1420.00;   (* tax brackets for single status *)
  SingBracket[2]:= 3910.00;
  SingBracket[3]:= 5200.00;
  SingBracket[4]:= 9400.00;
  SingBracket[5]:= 14000.00;
  SingBracket[6]:= 17200.00;
```

```
      SingBracket[7]:= 22500.00;
      SingBracket[8]:= 1E10;
      SingConst[1]:= 0.00;   (* base tax for income brackets (single) *)
      SingConst[2]:= 348.60;
      SingConst[3]:= 555.00;
      SingConst[4]:= 1353.00;
      SingConst[5]:= 2457.00;
      SingConst[6]:= 3385.00;
      SingConst[7]:= 5081.00;
      SingRate[1]:= 0.14; (* tax rates for single *)
      SingRate[2]:= 0.16;
      SingRate[3]:= 0.19;
      SingRate[4]:= 0.24;
      SingRate[5]:= 0.29;
      SingRate[6]:= 0.32;
      SingRate[7]:= 0.37;
end; (* initialize *)


procedure Conversion;

const
   maxexempt = 50;

var
   aberrant:integer;

begin
   repeat
      write('Number of pay periods per year: ')
   until ReadInt(period,1,365);
   repeat
      write('Number of withholding exemptions: ')
   until ReadInt(Nexempt,1,maxexempt);
   if period in [1,2,4,12,24,26,52] then
      case period of
         52:subtract:=Nexempt*19.23;
         26:subtract:=Nexempt*38.46;
         24:subtract:=Nexempt*41.66;
         12:subtract:=Nexempt*83.33;
          4:subtract:=Nexempt*250.0;
          2:subtract:=Nexempt*500.0;
          1:subtract:=Nexempt*1000.0
      end {  case }
    else
      begin
        repeat
          write('How many work days in the year: ')
        until ReadInt(aberrant,1,365);
        subtract:=Nexempt*aberrant * 3.85;
      end; {  if }
   AnnualTaxbl:=income * period - subtract;
end;


procedure married;

var
   w : integer;
```

```
begin
   conversion;
   if AnnualTaxbl<=MarBracket[1] then
      tax:=0.0
   else
     begin
       w:= 1;
       while AnnualTaxbl > MarBracket[w] do
         w:= w + 1;
       w:= w - 1;
       tax:= MarConst[w]+(MarRate[w])*(AnnualTaxbl - MarBracket[w])
     end
end;



procedure single;   { includes heads of household }

var
   w : integer;

begin
   conversion;
   if AnnualTaxbl <= SingBracket[1] then
      tax:=0.0
   else
     begin
       w:=1;
       while AnnualTaxbl > SingBracket[w] do
         w:=w + 1;
       w:= w - 1 ;
       tax:=SingConst[w]+(SingRate[w])*(AnnualTaxbl - SingBracket[w])
     end;
end;



procedure GetTaxData;

var
   maritalstatus:char;

begin
   repeat
      write('Current taxable pay: ')
   until ReadReal(income);
   repeat
      write('Year-to-date taxable pay: ')
   until ReadReal(YTDpay);
   repeat
      write('Marital status: (S=single   M=married) ');
      readln(maritalstatus)
   until maritalstatus in ['s','m','S','M'];
   case maritalstatus of
      's','S':single;
      'm','M':married;
      end; (* case *)
   end; {  gettaxdata }
```

```
procedure SocialSecurityTax;

const
    cutoffpt=32400;

var
    FICAtax:real;

begin
    writeln('Federal income tax withheld: ',tax/period);
    remainder:= AnnualTaxbl - tax;
    if YTDpay < cutoffpt then
        FICAtax:=(remainder * 0.0670)/period
    else
        FICAtax:=0.0;
    writeln('FICA tax = ',FICAtax);
end;


begin {  main }
    writeln;writeln('Federal Withholding Taxes');
    initialize;
    repeat
        writeln;
        GetTaxData;
        SocialSecurityTax;
    until NotAgain
end.
```

69
Tax Depreciation Schedule

This program tabulates annual depreciation amounts. You can use the sum of digits method or any declining balance percentage method. You must know the purchase price (initial value), salvage value at the end of the depreciable life, and the life of the item being depreciated. If you are doing declining balance depreciation, you must also know the percentage method.

Program Notes

The constant PageSize, when added to and subtracted from other quantities, controls the printing of a heading at the top of each page of output. If you are using exceptionally short or long paper, your output may not have the heading at the top of the page. Adjust the constant PageSize if this misalignment is serious. If your output device is set for automatic paging, you should decrease the value of the constant PageSize by an amount equal to the number of lines "skipped" by the automatic pagination.

Examples:

WJR Hardware Inc. put a new roof on their office building for $27,000.00. They expect to replace it in nine years. What would the annual depreciation amounts be using the sum of digits?

First National Bank built a new home office building for $1.2 million. Run a tax depreciation schedule on the building using 150% declining balance method with a 30-year life. Assume a salvage value of $250,000. You will notice that the depreciation falls below straight line ($31,666.67 per year) at year 9.

Run:

```
Tax Depreciation Schedule

Purchase price: 27000
Salvage value: 0
Life in years: 9
Method: Sum of digits
           or
       Declining balance (s/d): s


        Sum of Digits Tax Depreciation
              Price $ 27000.0
        Salvage Value $    0.00
    Net Depreciated $ 27000.0
           Life 9 years

YEAR        DEPRECIATION           BALANCE
1              5400.00             21600.0
2              4800.00             16800.0
3              4200.00             12600.0
4              3600.00             9000.00
5              3000.00             6000.00
6              2400.00             3600.00
7              1800.00             1800.00
8              1200.00              600.00
9               600.00               0.00
```

Would you like another run? (y/n) y

Purchase price: 1200000
Salvage value: 250000
Life in years: 30
Method: Sum of digits
              or
      Declining balance (s/d): d
Method in % 150

      Declining Balance Tax Depreciation
                Price $ 1.20000E6
         Salvage Value $ 250000.
      Net Depreciated $ 950000.
              Life 30 years
              Method 150%

YEAR	DEPRECIATION	BALANCE
1	47500.0	902500.
2	45125.0	857375.
3	42868.7	814506.
4	40725.3	773781.
5	38689.0	735092.
6	36754.6	698337.
7	34916.9	663420.
8	33171.0	630249.
9	31512.5	598737.
10	29936.8	568800.
11	28440.0	540360.
12	27018.0	513342.
13	25667.1	487675.
14	24383.7	463291.
15	23164.6	440127.
16	22006.3	418120.
17	20906.0	397214.
18	19860.7	377354.
19	18867.7	358486.
20	17924.3	340562.
21	17028.1	323534.
22	16176.7	307357.
23	15367.8	291989.
24	14599.4	277390.
25	13869.5	263520.
26	13176.0	250344.
27	12517.2	237827.
28	11891.3	225936.
29	11296.8	214639.
30	10731.9	203907.

Would you like another run? (y/n) n

Program Listing:

```
program TaxDepreciation(input,output);
const  PageSize = 66;

var  price, SalvageValue,
     NetDepreciated, percent: real;
     Years : integer;
     DecliningBalance : boolean;
```

198

```
{$I NotAgain}
{$I ReadReal }
{$I ReadInt }


procedure GetData;
var  method : char;
begin
  repeat
    repeat
      write('Purchase price: ')
    until ReadReal(price);
    repeat
      write('Salvage value: ')
    until  ReadReal(SalvageValue);
  until price > SalvageValue;
  NetDepreciated:= price - SalvageValue;
  repeat
    write('Life in years: ')
  until  ReadInt(Years,1,maxint);
  repeat
    writeln('Method: Sum of digits');
    writeln('or':15);
    write('    Declining balance (s/d): ');
    readln(method)
  until method in ['S','D','s','d'];
  DecliningBalance:= method in ['D','d'];
  if DecliningBalance then
    begin
      repeat
        write('Method in % ')
      until ReadReal(percent);
      percent:= percent/100
    end
end;  {  procedure GetData }


procedure PrintHeading(var line : integer);
var  h : integer;
begin
  for h:=line to PageSize do
    writeln;
  line:= 7;
  if DecliningBalance then
    write('   Declining Balance ')
  else  write('       Sum of Digits ');
  writeln('Tax Depreciation');
  writeln('Price $':22,price:7:2);
  writeln('Salvage Value $':22,SalvageValue:7:2);
  writeln('Net Depreciated $':22,NetDepreciated:7:2);
  writeln('Life ':17,Years,' years');
  if DecliningBalance then
    begin
      percent:= percent * 100;
      write('Method ':18);
      if percent= trunc(percent) then
        write(trunc(percent))
      else  write(percent:6:2);
      writeln('%');
      percent:= percent/100;
      line:= line + 1
    end;
```

```
    writeln;
    writeln('YEAR','DEPRECIATION':18,'BALANCE':17)
end;  {  procedure PrintHeading }


procedure CalculateDepreciation;
var RemainingBalance,
    Depreciation : real;
    CurrentYear,line,h : integer;

  procedure GetNextFigures;
  begin
    if DecliningBalance then
      Depreciation:= RemainingBalance * percent / Years
    else
      Depreciation:= 2 * NetDepreciated * (Years - CurrentYear + 1) /
                     ((Years + 1) * Years);
      RemainingBalance:= RemainingBalance - Depreciation
  end;  {  procedure GetNextFigures (inside CalculateDepreciation) }


begin
  if DecliningBalance then line:= 10
  else line:= 9;
  RemainingBalance:= NetDepreciated;
  for CurrentYear:=1 to Years do
    begin
      if (line > (PageSize - 11)) or (CurrentYear = 1) then
        PrintHeading(line);
      GetNextFigures;
      if RemainingBalance < 0 then
        begin
          writeln('Complete depreciation in year ',CurrentYear);
          CurrentYear:= years
        end
      else
        writeln(CurrentYear,Depreciation:18:2,RemainingBalance:20:2);
      line:= line+1
    end;
  for h:=line to PageSize do
    writeln
end; {  procedure CalculateDepreciation }


begin {  main }
  writeln;writeln('Tax Depreciation Schedule');
  repeat
    writeln;
    GetData;
    CalculateDepreciation
  until NotAgain
end.
```

70
Check Writer

This program prints a check if you provide the date in numeric form, the amount, and the payee. The program translates the amount into words and prints the check with appropriate spacing. If your checks do not conform exactly to the spacing the program provides, you can alter the spacing by making minor program modifications.

When the program asks the question "READY TO PRINT CHECK?", insert a blank check into your printing device. The check should be set one line above the line on which the date will be printed. Then answer "y" to the question, and the check will start printing.

Please note that the date is entered in numeric form, with one space separating each entry. You need only specify the final two digits of the year for dates in the 20th century.

Example:

Your corporation must print a check for $4975.89 to J. Austin and Associates and a check for Freida Alexander for $103.75.

Run:

```
Check Writer
Date: (MM DD YYYY) 3 8 77
Name of recipient: Freida Alexander
Whole dollars: $103
Cents: 75
Ready to print check? (y/n) y
```

```
                                                    NO. 382

HEAVENLY BANK
EMERYVILLE OFFICE
4120 ASHBY AVENUE                          MARCH 8    19 82
EMERYVILLE, CA 94601                       $ 103.75
                                 AMOUNT $  103.75


PAY TO THE ORDER OF        Freida Alexander


   one hundred three dollars and 75 cents


     MIRACLE CORPORATION
     1111 COUNTRY ROAD
     COUNTRYVILLE, CA 94132


                                      1328252158
```

```
Check Writer
Date: (MM DD YYYY) 3 8 77
Name of recipient: J. Austin & Associates
Whole dollars: $4975
Cents: 89
Ready to print check? (y/n) y
```

HEAVENLY BANK   NO. 328
EMERYVILLE OFFICE
4120 ASHBY AVENUE
EMERYVILLE, CA 94601
                                        MARCH 8   19 82
                                        $ 4975.89
                                        AMOUNT $ 4975.89

PAY TO THE ORDER OF   J. Austin & Associates

forty-nine hundred seventy-five dollars and 89 cents

MIRACLE CORPORATION
1111 COUNTRY ROAD
COUNTRYVILLE, CA 94132

                                        1328252158

Program Listing:

```
program CheckWriter(input, output);
const
   ToDate = 60;
   ToAmt = 60;
   ToName = 10;
   DateRoom = 11;
type
{$I dates}
{$I CharStrs}
   line = packed array[0..80] of char;
var
   d: date;
   name: CharStr;
   dollars, cents: integer;

{$I ReadInt}
{$I YesNotNo}
{$I LeapYear}
{$I ReadDate}
{$I GetStr}
{$I PutStr}

   procedure SpellNum(i: integer);
   begin
      if (i >= 10000) or (i >= 1000) and (i mod 1000 div 100 = 0) then
         begin
            SpellNum(i div 1000);
            write(' thousand ');
            SpellNum(i mod 1000)
         end
```

```
    else if i >= 100 then
      begin    ,
        SpellNum(i div 100);
        write(' hundred ');
        SpellNum(i mod 100)
      end
    else if i >= 20 then
      begin
        case i div 10 of
          2: write('twenty');
          3: write('thirty');
          4: write('forty');
          5: write('fifty');
          6: write('sixty');
          7: write('seventy');
          8: write('eighty');
          9: write('ninety')
        end; { case }
        if i mod 10 <> 0 then
          begin
            write('-');
            SpellNum(i mod 10)
          end
      end
    else if i in [14, 16..19] then
      begin
        SpellNum(i mod 10);
        write('teen')
      end
    else if i >= 10 then
      case i of
        10: write('ten');
        11: write('eleven');
        12: write('twelve');
        13: write('thirteen');
        15: write('fifteen');
      end { case }
    else if i > 0 then
      case i of
        1: write('one');
        2: write('two');
        3: write('three');
        4: write('four');
        5: write('five');
        6: write('six');
        7: write('seven');
        8: write('eight');
        9: write('nine')
      end { case }
end; { SpellNum }

procedure WriteDate(d:date);
var
  len: integer;
begin
  case d.month of
    1: write('January');
    2: write('February');
    3: write('March');
    4: write('April');
    5: write('May');
```

```
        6: write('June');
        7: write('July');
        8: write('August');
        9: write('September');
       10: write('October');
       11: write('November');
       12: write('December')
    end; { case }
    case d.month of
       5: len := 3;
       6, 7: len := 4;
       3, 4: len := 5;
       8: len := 6;
       1, 10: len := 7;
       2, 9, 11, 12: len := 8
    end;
    write(' ');
    write(d.day:0);
    if d.day > 10 then
       len := len + 3
    else
       len := len + 2;
    write(' ':DateRoom - len);
    write(d.year mod 100:0)
  end; { WriteDate }

begin { main }
  writeln('Check Writer');
  repeat
     write('Date: ')
  until ReadDate(d);
  write('Name of recipient: ');
  name := GetStr;
  repeat
     write('Whole dollars: $')
  until ReadInt(dollars, 0, maxint);
  repeat
     write('Cents: ')
  until ReadInt(cents, 0, maxint);
  repeat
     write('Ready to print check? (y/n) ')
  until YesNotNo;
  write(' ':ToDate);
  WriteDate(d);
  writeln;writeln;
  write(' ':ToAmt);
  write(dollars);
  write('.');
  if cents < 10 then
     write('0');
  writeln(cents:0);
  writeln;
  write(' ':ToName);
  PutStr(name);
  writeln;writeln;
  SpellNum(dollars);
  writeln(' dollars and ', cents:0, ' cents')
end.
```

71
Recipe Cost

This program calculates the total cost and the cost per serving of a recipe. For each ingredient, you provide the purchase price, the amount purchased, the amount used in the recipe, and the number of recipe units per purchase unit.

Example:

The recipe for strawberry shortcake calls for the ingredients listed below. Calculate the cost of the recipe and the cost per serving if the recipe feeds eight.

Strawberry Shortcake
8 servings

3 c. flour	2.5 c./lb	$1.59	5 lb.
3¼ tsp. baking powder	15 tsp./oz.	0.43	4 oz.
¼ c. sugar	2 c./lb.	1.24	5 lb.
1¼ tsp. salt	6 tsp./oz.	0.29	1 lb.
½ c. butter	2 c./lb.	1.49	1 lb.
1 egg	12/doz.	0.75	1 doz.
⅔ c. milk	4 c./qt.	0.40	1 qt.
3 pt. strawberries	–	0.49	1 pt.
½ pt. whipping cream	–	0.59	½ pt.

What would the cost per serving be if the recipe serves 12?

Run:

```
Recipe Cost

Number of ingredients: 9
Ingredient 1:
  Cost for bulk unit in store: $1.59
  Number of units in bulk: 5
  Number of recipe units per bulk unit: 2.5
  Number of recipe units called for: 3
Ingredient 2:
  Cost for bulk unit in store: $.43
  Number of units in bulk: 4
  Number of recipe units per bulk unit: 15
  Number of recipe units called for: 3.25
Ingredient 3:
  Cost for bulk unit in store: $1.24
  Number of units in bulk: 5
  Number of recipe units per bulk unit: 2
  Number of recipe units called for: .25
Ingredient 4:
  Cost for bulk unit in store: $.29
  Number of units in bulk: 1
  Number of recipe units per bulk unit: 96
  Number of recipe units called for: 1.25
```

```
Ingredient 5:
  Cost for bulk unit in store: $1.49
  Number of units in bulk: 1
  Number of recipe units per bulk unit: 2
  Number of recipe units called for: .5
Ingredient 6:
  Cost for bulk unit in store: $.75
  Number of units in bulk: 1
  Number of recipe units per bulk unit: 12
  Number of recipe units called for: 1
Ingredient 7:
  Cost for bulk unit in store: $.40
  Number of units in bulk: 1
  Number of recipe units per bulk unit: 4
  Number of recipe units called for: .666667
Ingredient 8:
  Cost for bulk unit in store: $.49
  Number of units in bulk: 1
  Number of recipe units per bulk unit: 1
  Number of recipe units called for: 3
Ingredient 9:
  Cost for bulk unit in store: $.59
  Number of units in bulk: 1
  Number of recipe units per bulk unit: 1
  Number of recipe units called for: 1
Number of servings: 8

Total cost for 1 recipe = $   3.00
Cost per serving = $ 0.38

Change number of servings? (y/n) y
Number of servings: 12

Total cost for 1 recipe = $   3.00
Cost per serving = $ 0.25

Change number of servings? (y/n) n
```

Program Listing:

```pascal
program recipe(input, output);
var
  NumIngreds, ingred: integer;
  cost, BulkCost, UnitsInBulk, RecInBulk, NumRecUnits, NumServs: real;

{$I ReadInt}
{$I ReadReal}
{$I YesNotNo}

begin { main }
  writeln('Recipe Cost');
  writeln;
  repeat
    write('Number of ingredients: ')
  until ReadInt(NumIngreds, 1, maxint);
  cost := 0.0;
  for ingred := 1 to NumIngreds do
    begin
      writeln('Ingredient ', ingred:0, ':');
      repeat
        write('  Cost for bulk unit in store: $')
```

```
        until ReadReal(BulkCost);
        repeat
          write('  Number of units in bulk: ')
        until ReadReal(UnitsInBulk);
        repeat
          write('  Number of recipe units per bulk unit: ')
        until ReadReal(RecInBulk);
        repeat
          write('  Number of recipe units called for: ')
        until ReadReal(NumRecUnits);
        cost := cost + BulkCost / UnitsInBulk / RecInBulk * NumRecUnits
      end; { for }
    repeat
      repeat
        write('Number of servings: ')
      until ReadReal(NumServs);
      writeln;
      writeln('Total cost for 1 recipe = $', cost:6:2);
      writeln('Cost per serving = $', cost / NumServs:5:2);
      writeln;
      write('Change number of servings? (y/n) ')
    until not YesNotNo
end.
```

72
Survey Check (Map Check)

Courtesy: Robert Irving
Northridge, California

This program calculates the error of closure and area of a plot for which a traverse of the perimeter is available. The program will also calculate how far North and East the end of an open traverse is from its origin (the Northing and Easting). The local coordinates of the origin can be entered for an open traverse. Negative values of Northing and Easting are South and West, respectively, of the 0,0 origin of the survey.

The individual legs of the traverse may be either straight lines or arcs of circles. To compute the traverse, you must have the bearing and length of each straight leg. You also need the radius, bearing of chord, and length of chord (or radius, arc measure, and bearing of a tangent) for each curved leg.

For a closed survey, pick any intersection of legs as a starting point, and number the lines and arcs, starting with 1, in a *clockwise* direction around the perimeter. If any arc is 180 degrees or more, it must be broken into smaller arcs, each less than 180 degrees.

By convention, surveyors measure bearings East and West of North and South, as shown in the following figure. This convention was established in the days before computers, so that trigonometric functions could be easily looked up in tables not exceeding 90 degrees. For each leg, you must enter the quadrant number and the degrees, minutes, and seconds East or West of the North-South axis. The program will indicate the direction of the leg (e.g., SW), and will convert the quadrant, degrees, etc. to an azimuth angle. Azimuth is measured clockwise from North to 360 degrees.

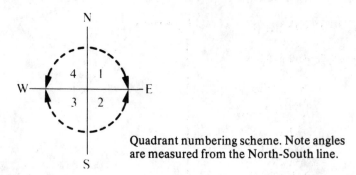

Quadrant numbering scheme. Note angles are measured from the North-South line.

A curved leg, or arc, is defined by two auxiliary legs, each of which is a radius of the arc. The bearing of the first auxiliary leg is the direction of the radius from the first encountered end of the arc to the center of the arc. You can compute this bearing from the bearing of the arc's tangent at that point, since the radius is perpendicular to the tangent. The survey may show the bearing of the tangent. If not, you can compute it by adding one half the angular extent of the arc to the bearing of the arc's chord, as shown in the next figure.

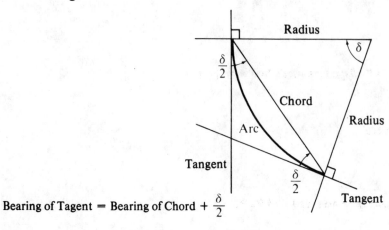

Bearing of Tagent = Bearing of Chord + $\frac{\delta}{2}$

The bearing of the second radius is from the center of the arc to the other end, and the distance is entered as a *negative* number to signal to the computer that this and the prior leg are not perimeter legs, but auxiliary legs of an arc.

The program asks you for the bearing and distance of each leg by number. Legs are entered in sets of ten (or less). Following the last entry in a set, you can correct any leg in the set. You must enter both auxiliary legs of an arc in the same set. You can enter a bearing of zero to end one set, and then enter more legs on the next set.

When you have corrected a set, a traverse table is printed for the set. This includes each leg number, direction, azimuth angle and distance, and incremental and cumulative Northing and Easting. The cumulative Northing and Easting after the last leg on a closed survey gives the error of closure. Arc angle, radius, sector area, chord length, and tangent length are printed between the two auxiliary legs of each curved leg.

Following the printout of the last leg of a closed survey, the area of the plot will be printed, both in square feet and in acres. The area computed is very accurate provided two conditions are met:

1. The error of closure is small (0.01 feet is usual for a house lot), and

2. The area is sufficiently small that curvature of the earth does not become significant. Surveys covering several tens of miles have to account for this latter factor.

Example:

The figure below illustrates the boundaries of a lot with one curved side. The leg numbers are circled. Bearings and distances are shown for each leg. Find the error of closure and lot area.

1. S39°0′0″E
   149.83
2. S39°0′0″E
   50.00
3. N85°23′53″W
   50.00
4. N85°23′53″W
   114.32
5. N1°5′0″E
   132.78
6. N46°0′0″E
   14.00
7. S89°0′0″E
   25.46

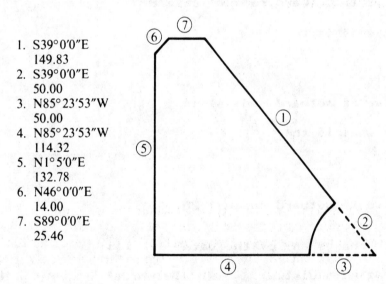

Run:

```
Map Survey Check


Is survey open or closed? ("c"=closed, "o"=open) c

How many Legs? 7

For Leg number 1 what is the
Quadrant: 2
Degrees: 39
Minutes: 0
Seconds: 0
Distance (Negative if outward radius) 149.83
```

For Leg number 2 what is the
Quadrant: 2
Degrees: 39
Minutes: 0
Seconds: 0
Distance (Negative if outward radius) 50

For Leg number 3 what is the
Quadrant: 4
Degrees: 85
Minutes: 23
Seconds: 53
Distance (Negative if outward radius) -50

For Leg number 4 what is the
Quadrant: 4
Degrees: 85
Minutes: 23
Seconds: 53
Distance (Negative if outward radius) 114.32

For Leg number 5 what is the
Quadrant: 1
Degrees: 1
Minutes: 5
Seconds: 0
Distance (Negative if outward radius) 132.78

For Leg number 6 what is the
Quadrant: 1
Degrees: 46
Minutes: 0
Seconds: 0
Distance (Negative if outward radius) 14

For Leg number 7 what is the
Quadrant: 2
Degrees: 89
Minutes: 0
Seconds: 0
Distance (Negative if outward radius) 25.46

Would you like to change any of the data? (y/n) n

Leg/Dir.		Azimuth/Dist.				Del N/Del E		Northing/Easting	
								0.000 /	0.000
1	SE	141	0	0 /	149.830	-116.439 /	94.293	-116.439 /	94.293
2	SE	141	0	0 /	50.000	-38.857 /	31.467	-155.295 /	125.759
	Arc:	46	23	53	R= 50.000	A= 2024.50	C= 39.392	T= 21.429	
3	NW	274	36	7 /	50.000	4.010 /	-49.839	-151.285 /	75.920
4	NW	274	36	7 /	114.320	9.169 /	-113.952	-142.116 /	-38.031
5	NE	1	5	0 /	132.780	132.756 /	2.510	-9.359 /	-35.521
6	NE	46	0	0 /	14.000	9.725 /	10.071	0.366 /	-25.450
7	SE	91	0	0 /	25.460	-0.444 /	25.456	-0.078 /	0.006

Would you like to see more Legs? (y/n) n

Plot Area is   13347.7   Square Feet

SURVEY CHECK (MAP CHECK)

```
Plot Area is  0.30642 Acres

Would you like another run? (y/n) n
```

Program Listing:

```
program Map(input,output);
uses transcend; {omit if not Apple Pascal}

const
 PI=3.14159;
 MaxLegSet=10;
 ConvertRad=1.74532E-2;

type
 index=1..MaxLegSet;
 Cordarray=array[index] of real;

var
 NumLeg:index;
 Legs,Bearing:Cordarray;
 Northing,Easting:real;
 Area:real;
 Response:char;

{$I ReadInt}
{$I NotAgain}


procedure NegDistance(i:index);
var
 Distance:real;

begin
write('Distance (Negative if outward radius) ');
readln(Distance);
Legs[i]:=Distance;
if (Distance <= 0)  and (i > 1) then
   if abs(Distance) <> abs(Legs[i-1]) then
      NegDistance(i)
end;   {procedure NegDistance}


procedure ReadDeg(i:index);
const
 LastQuad=4;
 MaxDeg=360;
 MaxMin=60;
 MaxSec=MaxMin;

var
 Quad,Deg,Min,Sec:integer;

begin
writeln;
writeln('For Leg number ',i,' what is the ');
repeat
   write('Quadrant: ');
until ReadInt(Quad,1,LastQuad);
```

```
repeat
   write('Degrees: ');
until ReadInt(Deg,0,MaxDeg);
repeat
    write('Minutes: ');
until ReadInt(Min,0,MaxMin);
repeat
    write('Seconds: ');
until ReadInt(Sec,0,MaxSec);
Bearing[i]:=Deg + (Min + Sec / MaxSec) / MaxMin;
if Bearing[i] > 90 then begin
   writeln('Incorrect values for Leg ',i);
   ReadDeg(i)
   end;
case Quad of
  1:NegDistance(i);
  2:begin
    Bearing[i]:=180 - Bearing[i];
    NegDistance(i)
    end;
  3:begin
    Bearing[i]:=Bearing[i] + 180;
    NegDistance(i)
    end;
  4:begin
    Bearing[i]:=360 - Bearing[i];
    NegDistance(i)
    end
  end {case}
end;   {procedure ReadDeg}

procedure ReadData;
var
 answer:char;
 i,Change:index;

begin
  Northing:=0;
  Easting:=0;
  answer:=' ';
  while not (answer in ['c','C','O','o']) do begin
   write('Is survey open or closed? ("c"=closed, "o"=open) ');
   readln(answer);
   if answer in ['o','O'] then begin
      write('Origin Northing: ');
      readln(Northing);
      write('Origin Easting: ');
      readln(Easting)
      end   {if answer}
   end;   {while not etc.}
  writeln;
  repeat
    write('How many Legs? ');
  until ReadInt(NumLeg,1,MaxLegSet);
  for i:= 1 to NumLeg do
    ReadDeg(i);
  answer:='y';
  while answer in ['y','Y'] do begin
    writeln;write('Would you like to change any of the data? (y/n) ');
    readln(answer);
    if answer in ['y','Y'] then begin
```

```
      repeat
          write('Which   Leg would you like to change? ');
      until ReadInt(Change,1,NumLeg);
      ReadDeg(Change)
      end  {if answer}
   end  {while answer}
end;  {procedure ReadData}


function tan(N:real):real;
var
 Temp:real;

begin
if (N = PI/4) or (N = 2*PI/3) then
    Temp:=0
else
    Temp:=sin(N)/cos(N);
tan:=Temp
end;  {function Tangent}


procedure BreakDown(var Degrees,Minutes,Seconds:integer; Number:real);
var
 TempMin:real;

begin
  Degrees:=trunc(Number);
  TempMin:=((Number - Degrees) * 60);
  Minutes:=trunc(TempMin);
  Seconds:=round((TempMin - Minutes) * 60)
end;  {procedure BreakDown}


procedure Arcing(count:index);
var
 AreaOne,Tangent,Constant,TempBearing,CurveOne:real;
 Degrees,Minutes,Seconds:integer;

begin
  Constant:=abs(Bearing[count]-Bearing[count-1]);
  Constant:=abs(180 - Constant);
  Legs[count]:=(-Legs[count]);
  AreaOne:=(Constant/180)*PI*sqr(Legs[count]);
  CurveOne:=2 * Legs[count] * sin(Constant/2 * ConvertRad);
  Tangent:=Legs[count] * tan(Constant/2 * ConvertRad);
  TempBearing:=Bearing[count] - Bearing[count-1];
  if (TempBearing > 180) and ((TempBearing>=(-180))
              or (TempBearing<=0)) then
     Area:=Area + AreaOne
  else
     Area:=Area - AreaOne;
  BreakDown(Degrees,Minutes,Seconds,Constant);
  write('      Arc: ',Degrees:3,'  ',Minutes:2,'  ',Seconds:2);
  write('     R= ',Legs[count]:1:3,' ',' A= ',AreaOne:1:3,
          ' C= ',CurveOne:1:3);
  writeln('   T= ',Tangent:1:3);
  writeln
end;  {procedure Arcing}
```

```pascal
   procedure Calculate;
   var
   count:index;
   Distance,Length:real;
   Degrees,Minutes,Seconds:integer;

begin
writeln;
write('Leg/Dir.          Azimuth/Dist.                ');
writeln('      Del N/Del E            Northing/Easting');
write('                                                          ');
writeln('                          ',Northing:8:3,' /',Easting:3:3);
writeln;
Area:=0;
for count:= 1 to NumLeg do begin
   if Legs[count] < 0 then
      Arcing(count);
   Length:=Legs[count] * cos(Bearing[count] * ConvertRad);
   Distance:=Legs[count] * sin(Bearing[count] * ConvertRad);
   Northing:=Northing + Length;
   Easting:=Easting + Distance;
   Area:=Area - (Easting * Length) + (Northing * Distance);
   write(count,' ');
   if (Bearing[count] = 0) or (Bearing[count] = 0) then write ('N')
   else if Bearing[count] < 90 then write(' NE')
   else if Bearing[count] = 90 then write('  E')
   else if Bearing[count] < 180 then write(' SE')
   else if Bearing[count] = 180 then write('  S')
   else if Bearing[count] < 270 then write(' SW')
   else if Bearing[count] = 270 then write('  W')
   else write(' NW');
   BreakDown(Degrees,Minutes,Seconds,Bearing[count]);
   write('      ',Degrees:3,' ',Minutes:2,' ',Seconds:2,' ');
   write('/',Legs[count]:8:3,'              ',Length:8:3);
   write(' /',Distance:8:3,'            ',Northing:8:3,' /',Easting:8:3);
   writeln
   end  {for count}
end;  {procedure Calculate}

begin {Main}
writeln;writeln('Map Survey Check');writeln;writeln;
repeat
   ReadData;
   Response:='y';
   while Response in ['y','Y'] do begin
      Calculate;
      writeln;
      write('Would you like to see more Legs? (y/n) ');
      readln(Response)
      end;  {while Response}
   Area:=abs(Area/2);
   writeln;writeln('Plot Area is ',Area:1:5,' square feet. ');
   writeln;
   writeln('Plot Area is ',(Area/4.356E4 * 1E8)/1E8:1:5,' acres. ');
   writeln;
until NotAgain
end.  {Main}
```

73
Day of the Week

This program calculates the day of the week that a particular date falls on. You must enter the date in numeric form in this order: month, day, year. Spaces must separate the figures.

Examples:

Maggie's birthdate is March 4, 1953. On what day of the week was she born?

Bryan made a long distance phone call on September 30, 1977. He claims that he was overcharged for the call because he was billed at the prime time weekday rate. On what day of the week did he make the call?

Run:

```
Day Of The Week

date: (MM DD YYYY) 3 4 1953
Wednesday
Would you like another run? (y/n) y

date: (MM DD YYYY) 9 30 1977
Friday
Would you like another run? (y/n) n
```

Program Listing:

```
program DayOfTheWeek(input, output);
type
{$I dates}
var
  d: date;

{$I LeapYear}
{$I ReadDate}
{$I NotAgain}

  function DayOfWeek(d: date): integer;
  var
    m: integer;
  begin
    with d do
      begin
        if month > 2 then
          m := month
        else
          begin
            m := month + 12;
            year := year - 1
          end;
        DayOfWeek := (day + 2 * m + trunc(0.6 * (m + 1)) + year
                  + year div 4 - year div 100 + year div 400 + 2) mod 7
      end
  end;
```

```
begin { main }
  writeln('Day Of The Week');
  repeat
    writeln;
    write('date: ');
    while not ReadDate(d) do
      write('Invalid date, date: ');
    case DayOfWeek(d) of
      0: write('Saturday');
      1: write('Sunday');
      2: write('Monday');
      3: write('Tuesday');
      4: write('Wednesday');
      5: write('Thursday');
      6: write('Friday')
    end; { case }
    writeln;
  until NotAgain
end.
```

74
Days Between Two Dates

This program calculates the number of days between two dates. It assumes that there is a one day difference between today and yesterday and between today and tomorrow. The program takes leap years into account in its calculations. Naturally, the number of the month must not exceed 12 and the number of the day must not exceed the number of days in the month in question.

Please keep the following guidelines in mind as you use the program:

1. You must enter the earlier date first.

2. You must enter dates in "month, day, year" numeric format with spaces separating each component of an entry.

A violation of these rules will earn you an "Invalid Date" message.

Example:

Socorro's birthdate is August 8, 1951. How many days old was she on her 30th birthday?

Run:

```
Days Between Two Dates

1st Date: (MM DD YYYY) 8 8 1951
2nd Date: (MM DD YYYY) 8 8 1981
Difference = 10958

Would you like another run? (y/n) n
```

Program Listing:

```
program DaysBetweenTwoDates(input, output);
type
{$I dates}
var
  c: char;
  date1, date2: date;

{$I LeapYear}
{$I ReadDate}
{$I DaysAbs}
{$I NotAgain}

begin { main }
  writeln('Days Between Two Dates');
  writeln;
  repeat
    write('1st Date: ');
    while not ReadDate(date1) do
      write('Invalid date, 1st Date = ');
    write('2nd Date: ');
    while not ReadDate(date2) do
```

```
      write('Invalid date, 2nd Date = ');
    writeln('Difference = ',
            DaysAbs(date2, yCorrect) - DaysAbs(date1, yCorrect):0);
    writeln
  until NotAgain
end.
```

75
Anglo to Metric

This program converts a measure given in anglo units to metric units. The conversions available in this program are as follows:

1   Inches to centimeters
2   Feet to centimeters
3   Feet to meters
4   Yards to meters
5   Miles to kilometers
6   Teaspoons to cubic centimeters
7   Tablespoons to cubic centimeters
8   Cups to liters
9   Pints to liters
10   Quarts to liters
11   Gallons to liters
12   Bushels to liters
13   Pecks to liters
14   Ounces to grams
15   Pounds to kilograms
16   Tons to kilograms
17   Degrees Fahrenheit to degrees Celsius

You must know the value of the anglo measurement and the number of the conversion (1-17 as listed above).

Program Notes

You can modify this program to convert any measurement from one system to another, including metric to English, if you follow these steps carefully:

1. In procedure "Conversion," find the case label for the conversion that you want to replace with a new conversion. In the statement that follows the label, the variable "ConvertedValue" (the new value) is defined in terms of the variable "Value" (the value you input). Substitute your new equation, defining "ConvertedValue" in terms of "Value" with a new conversion factor.

2. In the procedure "PrintConvert," find the statement that corresponds to the same conversion you redefined in procedure "Conversion"; the statement will have the same case label. Substitute the names of your new units and you're ready to run!

Example:

Perform the following conversions:

8.5   miles to kilometers
75°   Fahrenheit to degrees Celsius
10   gallons to liters

Run:

```
Anglo to Metric Conversions

Which conversion do you need (1-17):  5
Value to be converted:  8.5
 8.50000 miles =  1.36765E1 kilometers.
```

```
Would you like another run? (y/n) y

Which conversion do you need (1-17):  16
Value to be converted:  765
 7.65000E2 tons =  6.94008E5 kilograms.
Would you like another run? (y/n) y

Which conversion do you need (1-17):  11
Value to be converted:  10
 1.00000E1 gallons =  3.78500E1 liters.
Would you like another run? (y/n) n
```

Program Listing:

```pascal
Program UnitsConversion(input,output);
var   cn:integer;
      Value, ConvertedValue:real;

{$I NotAgain}


procedure Conversion;

begin
  write('Which conversion do you need (1-17):   ');
  readln(cn);
  write('Value to be converted:   ');
  readln(Value);

  case cn of
    1: ConvertedValue := Value * 2.540;
    2: ConvertedValue := Value * 30.480;
    3: ConvertedValue := Value * 0.3048;
    4: ConvertedValue := Value * 0.9144;
    5: ConvertedValue := Value * 1.609;
    6: ConvertedValue := Value * 4.929;
    7: ConvertedValue := Value * 14.788;
    8: ConvertedValue := Value * 0.2366;
    9: ConvertedValue := Value * 0.4732;
    10: ConvertedValue := Value * 0.9463;
    11: ConvertedValue := Value * 3.785;
    12: ConvertedValue := Value * 35.24;
    13: ConvertedValue := Value * 8.809;
    14: ConvertedValue := Value * 28.3495;
    15: ConvertedValue := Value * 0.4536;
    16: ConvertedValue := Value * 907.2;
    17: ConvertedValue := (Value-32) * 5/9

  end
end; (* procedure conversion *)
procedure PrintConvert;

  procedure SecondHalfPrintConvert;
  begin
    case cn of
      9:Writeln(Value,' pints = ',ConvertedValue,' liters.');
      10:Writeln(Value,' quarts = ',ConvertedValue,' liters.');
      11:Writeln(Value,' gallons = ',ConvertedValue,' liters.');
      12:Writeln(Value,' bushels = ',ConvertedValue,' liters.');
      13:Writeln(Value,' pecks = ',ConvertedValue,' liters.');
```

```
        14:Writeln(Value,' ounces = ',ConvertedValue,' grams.');
        15:Writeln(Value,' pounds = ',ConvertedValue,' kilograms.');
        16:Writeln(Value,' tons = ',ConvertedValue,' kilograms.');
        17:Writeln(Value,' degrees F. = ',ConvertedValue,' degrees C.')
      end
  end;  (* procedure SecondHalfConvertPrint *)


  begin
    if cn <= 8 then
      case cn of
        1:Writeln(Value,' inches = ',ConvertedValue,' centimeters.');
        2:Writeln(Value,' feet = ',ConvertedValue,' centimeters.');
        3:Writeln(Value,' feet = ',ConvertedValue,' meters.');
        4:Writeln(Value,' yards = ',ConvertedValue,' meters.');
        5:Writeln(Value,' miles = ',ConvertedValue,' kilometers.');
        6:Writeln(Value,' tsp. = ',ConvertedValue,' cubic centimeters.');
        7:Writeln(Value,' tbsp. = ',ConvertedValue,' cubic centimeters.');
        8:Writeln(Value,' cups = ',ConvertedValue,' liters.');
      end
    else SecondHalfPrintConvert
  end; (* procedure PrintConvert *)


begin {main}
  Writeln('Anglo to Metric Conversions');
  Repeat
    writeln;
    Conversion;
    PrintConvert
  until NotAgain
end.
```

76
Alphabetize

This program alphabetizes a list of words, phrases or numbers, in ascending or descending order.

Numbers may be part of an alphanumeric phrase. However, they will not be put into numeric order unless they contain the same number of digits. Numbers with fewer digits must be justified to the right by prefixing zeros. Thus, if the numbers you are sorting range into the hundreds, the number 13 would be entered as 013.

Program Notes

The program will alphabetize and print results in A to Z order. If you want to sort from Z to A, make two changes in procedure "QuickSort." In the statement "while list[hi] > list[lo] do", change the ">" to a "<". In the statement "while list[lo] < list[hi] do", change the "<" to a ">".

To sort more than 25 items, change the constant "MaxObjects."

Examples:

Sort the following list of writers and artists from A to Z.

Barbara Chase-Ribaud
Alice Walker
Doris Lessing
Ursula Kroeber LeGuin
Maxine Hong Kingston
Sandra Chase
Margaret Atwood
Nicole Hollander
Zora Neale Hurston
Valerie J. Matsumoto
Margaret Walker
Vonda McIntyre

The scores on a math test range from 82 to 117. Put the scores in order, from highest to lowest.

89
102
111
100
99
117
102
82
97
91
108

Run:

```
Alphabetize

Number of items: 12
item 1: Chase-Ribaud Barbara
item 2: Walker Alice
item 3: Lessing Doris
```

```
item 4: LeGuin Ursula K.
item 5: Kingston Maxine Hong
item 6: Chase Sandra
item 7: Atwood Margaret
item 8: Hollander Nicole
item 9: Hurston Zora Neale
item 10: Matsumoto Valerie J.
item 11: Walker Margaret
item 12: McIntyre Vonda

Atwood Margaret
Chase Sandra
Chase-Ribaud Barbara
Hollander Nicole
Hurston Zora Neale
Kingston Maxine Hong
LeGuin Ursula K.
Lessing Doris
Matsumoto Valerie J.
McIntyre Vonda
Walker Alice
Walker Margaret
Would you like another run? (y/n) y


Alphabetize

Number of items: 11
item 1: 089
item 2: 102
item 3: 111
item 4: 100
item 5: 099
item 6: 117
item 7: 102
item 8: 082
item 9: 097
item 10: 091
item 11: 108

082
089
091
097
099
100
102
102
108
111
117
Would you like another run? (y/n) n
```

Program Listing:

```
program Alphabetize(input,output);
const  MaxObjects = 25;

type  object = string[20];
```

```
var   list : array[1..MaxObjects] of object;
      hold : object;
      NumObject : integer;

{$I ReadInt }
{$I NotAgain }

procedure ReadInput;
var  j : integer;

begin
  repeat
    write('Number of items: ')
  until ReadInt(NumObjects, 1, MaxObjects);
  for j:=1 to NumObjects do
    begin
      write('item ',j:0,': ');
      readln(list[j])
    end;
end;  { procedure ReadInput }

procedure QuickSort(low, high : integer);
var  lo, hi : integer;

begin
  lo:= low;
  hi:=high;
  repeat
    while list[hi] > list[lo] do
      hi:=hi - 1;
    if lo < hi then
      begin
        hold:= list[lo];
        list[lo]:= list[hi];
        list[hi]:= hold;
        lo:= lo + 1;
        while list[lo] < list[hi] do
          lo:=lo + 1;
        if lo < hi then
          begin
            hold:= list[lo];
            list[lo]:= list[hi];
            list[hi]:= hold;
          end;
      end;
  until lo = hi;
  if high - lo > 1 then
    QuickSort(lo + 1, high);
  if hi - low > 1 then
    QuickSort(low, hi-1);
end;  { procedure QuickSort }

procedure PrintResults;
var  j : 1..MaxObjects;
begin
  for j:=1 to NumObjects do
    writeln(list[j]);
end;  { procedure PrinResults }
```

```
begin  { main }
  writeln; writeln('Alphabetize');
  writeln;
  repeat
    ReadInput;
    QuickSort(1, NumObjects);
    writeln;
    PrintResults
  until NotAgain;
end.
```

A
Common Tools

Program development and maintenance are often more tedious and time-consuming than they need to be. Some of the components of a program may be functions that are common to many or all programs. A function which reads characters to a string is an example. Instead of coding these low-level functions dozens of times in dozens of ways, you could keep a collection of functions, procedures, and type declarations that represent the best solution to a series of common problems. Then particular solutions (or tools) could be called from the collection whenever needed. That is what we have done with the programs in this book. Each program calls one or more tools.

The 18 functions, procedures, and type declarations presented here and in Appendix B will mean substantial savings in time as you type in your programs. In addition, they will make your programs clearer and more understandable. You should decide what tools you will need for the programs you want to run, then type each tool into a separate file. These files are called "Include" files.

The Include files will be compiled as they are referenced in the program, and will appear on your terminal screen in the list of functions and procedures as your program compiles. Your computer writes a copy of each Include file into the program which included it, so the total size of the program reflects the size of the Include files as well as the remainder of the program.

When you run your program, "{$I" followed by the filename includes any of the files that the program needs. Each program listing shows the Include files needed by the program. Make sure Include files are on the same volume as the program that calls them. What appear to be comment delimiters ({ }) are actually an integral part of the Include file syntax. Don't omit them.

A comment section precedes the code in each tool. While reading the explanations, remember that "iff" is mathematical shorthand meaning "if and only if."

Tool A-1

```
{ Try to read a real number expressing a percent.  Return
  true iff successful.  If successful, return the number
  as a fraction through the var parameter p }
function GetPercent(var p: real): boolean;
begin
  write(': (%) ');
  GetPercent := true;
  if ReadReal(p) then
    p := p / 100
  else
    GetPercent := false
end; { GetPercent }
```

Tool A-2

```
{ Attempt to read a valid date.  Return true iff successful.
  Return any valid date read in the var parameter dat. }
function ReadDate(var dat: date): boolean;
var
  m, d, y: integer;

  function ValidDate(d: date): boolean;
  begin
    with d do
```

```
             ValidDate := (day <= 31) and (montn in [1, 3, 5, 7, 8, 10, 12])
                       or (day <= 30) and (month in [4, 6, 9, 11])
                       or (day <= 28) and (month = 2)
                       or (day = 29) and LeapYear(year)
          end; { ValidDate }

begin { ReadDate }
  write('(MM DD YYYY) ');
  readln(m, d, y);
  if y < 100 then
    y := y + 1900;
  if (m in [1..12]) and (d in [1..31]) and (y >= 1) then
    with dat do
      begin
        day := d;
        month := m;
        year := y;
        ReadDate := ValidDate(dat)
      end
  else
    ReadDate := false
end; { ReadDate }
```

Tool A-3

```
{ Solicit the user for either a y or an n (in either case), beeping
  at him or her until satisfied.  Return true iff a y was typed. }
function YesNotNo:boolean;
var
  c: char;
begin
  readln(c);
  while not (c in ['y', 'n', 'Y', 'N']) do
    begin
      write('Please type y for yes or n for no: ');
      readln(c)
    end;
  YesNotNo := c in ['y', 'Y']
end; { YesNotNo }
```

Tool A-4

```
{ see if the user would like to rerun the program }
function NotAgain: boolean;
var
  c: char;
begin
  write('Would you like another run? (y/n) ');
  readln(c);
  while not (c in ['y','Y','n','N']) do
    begin
      write('Type y for yes, or n for no: ');
      readln(c)

    end;
  NotAgain := c in ['n', 'N']
end; { NotAgain }
```

Tool A-5

```
{ return true iff y is a leap year }
function LeapYear(y: years): boolean;
begin
   LeapYear := (y mod 4 = 0) and ((y mod 400 = 0) or not (y mod 100 = 0))
end; { LeapYear }
```

Tool A-6

```
{ Round a real number to digits decimal places to the
  right of the decimal point.  Negative digits round
  to the left of the decimal point. }
function RealRound(num: real; digits: integer): real;
begin
   if num >= 0 then
     RealRound := RealTrunc(num + 0.5 * IntRaise(10, -digits), digits)
   else
     RealRound := RealTrunc(num - 0.5 * IntRaise(10, -digits), digits)
end; { RealRound }
```

Tool A-7

```
{  Truncate a real number to digits decimal places.  Negative
   digits truncates to the left of the decimal point. }
function RealTrunc(num: real; digits: integer): real;
const
   epsilon = 0.0000001;     { epsilon must be set for your implementation
                              of Pascal.  Run the program FindEpsilon and
                              plug in the value it tells you here. }
var
   accum: real;
   negate: boolean;
   digit, exp: integer;
begin
   negate := num < 0;
   if negate then
     num := - num;
   exp := 0;
   {Normalize number to be in less than 1}
   while num >= 1 do
     begin
       num := num / 10;
       exp := exp + 1;
       digits := digits + 1
     end;
   if digits <= 0 then
     RealTrunc := 0.0
   else

     begin
       accum := 0;
       while digits > 0 do
         begin
           num := num * 10;
           digit := trunc(num + epsilon);
           num := num - digit;
           accum := accum * 10 + digit;
           exp := exp - 1;
```

```
            digits := digits - 1
          end;
      while exp > 0 do
        begin
          accum := accum * 10;
          exp := exp - 1
        end;
      while exp < 0 do
        begin
          accum := accum / 10;
          exp := exp + 1
        end;
      if negate then
        accum := - accum;
      RealTrunc := accum
    end
end; { RealTrunc }
```

Tool A-8

```
{ raise a real number to an integer exponent }
function IntRaise(base: real; expt: integer): real;
begin
  if expt = 0 then
    IntRaise := 1
  else if expt < 0 then
    IntRaise := 1 / IntRaise(base, - expt)
  else
    if odd(expt) then
      IntRaise := IntRaise(base, expt - 1) * base
    else
      IntRaise := sqr(IntRaise(base, expt div 2))
end; { IntRaise }
```

Tool A-9

```
{ Raise a real base to a real exponent. }
function RealRaise(base, power: real): real;
begin
  if power = 0 then
    RealRaise := 1.0
  else if power < 0 then
    RealRaise := 1 / RealRaise(base, -power)
  else
    RealRaise := exp( power * ln(base) )
end; { RealRaise }
```

Tool A-10

```
{ DaysAbs returns the number of days from January 1, 1920
  until the given date, using the given calendar system.
  On computers using 16 bit arithmetic, this routine will
  work for dates for the rest of the century. }
function DaysAbs(d: date; kind: YearKinds): integer;
var
  days: integer;
```

```
begin
  with d do
    if (year < 1920) or (year > 1999) then
      writeln('ERROR: date out of range!')
    else if kind = y360m30 then
      DaysAbs := (year - 1920) * 360 + month * 30 + day
    else
      begin
        year := year - 1920;
        case month of
            1: days :=   0;  2: days :=  31;  3: days :=  59;
            4: days :=  90;  5: days := 120;  6: days := 151;
            7: days := 181;  8: days := 212;  9: days := 243;
           10: days := 273; 11: days := 304; 12: days := 334
        end;
        days := days + year * 365 + year div 4 + 1 + day;
        if (year mod 4 = 0) and (month <= 2) then
          days := days - 1;
        DaysAbs := days
      end
end; { DaysAbs }
```

Tool A-11

```
{ Stop so the user can read the screen.  Resume when the user
  types carriage return or newline. }
procedure pause;
begin
  write('Press return to continue');
  readln
end; { pause }
```

Tool A-12

```
{ Define a date to be a year, a month and a day.  Also
  notice the two different kinds of financial years, and
  the one kind of true year. }
YearKinds = (yCorrect, y360m30, y365y366);
years = 0..maxint;
date = record
         day: 1..31;
         month: 1..12;
         year: years
       end;
```

B
Common Implementations

Interactive input has always been a problem in Pasal, and different implementations of Pascal are idiosyncratic in their ways of handling interactive input. The functions, procedures, and data types in this appendix should help your programs to run on any of the common Pascal implementations.

The tools ReadInt and ReadReal read integer and real values respectively. Other Include files are for use with character and string values.

Tool B-1

```
{  Read a single character in the given set and return it.  Beep
   at the user for any character not in the set and keep reading
   until a valid character is given.  Where there is no confusion,
   accept alphabetic characters in either case. }
function read1char(okchars: CharSet): char;
const
  ordBEL = 7; { BEL is the ASCII character that rings the bell }
var
  c: char;
begin
  repeat
    readln(c);
    if not (c in okchars) then
      if c in ['A'..'Z'] then
        c := chr( ord(c) - ord('A') + ord('a') )
      else if c in ['a'..'z'] then
        c := chr( ord(c) - ord('a') + ord('A') );
    if not (c in okchars) then
        write(chr(ordBEL))
  until c in okchars;
  read1char := c
end; { read1char }
```

Tool B-2

```
{ read the rest of the current input line into a character string }
{ UCSD Pascal version }
function GetStr: CharStr;
const
  ordBS = 8;
var
  c: char;
  node: CharStr;
  backup: boolean;
begin
  repeat
    backup := false; { initial assumption }
    read(c);
    if eoln then
```

233

```
      begin
        GetStr := nil;
        readln
      end
    else if ord(c) = ordBS then
      begin
        write(' ', chr(ordBS));
        GetStr := nil
      end
    else
      begin
        if not backup then
          new(node);
        node^.data := c;
        node^.next := GetStr;
        if ord(input^) = ordBS then
          backup := true
        else
          GetStr := node
      end
  until not backup
end; { GetStr }
```

Tool B-3

```
{ define a character string to be a linked list of characters }
CharStr = ^ChrStrNode;
ChrStrNode = record
               data: char;
               next: CharStr
             end;
```

Tool B-4

```
{ write a character string on output }
procedure PutStr(s: CharStr);
begin
  if s <> nil then
    begin
      write(s^.data);
      PutStr(s^.next)
    end
end; { PutStr }
```

Tool B-5

```
{ Attempt to read an integer between low and high.  Return true
  and the integer (though i) iff successful. }
function ReadInt(var i: integer; low, high: integer): boolean;
begin
  i := 0;
  while not eoln and not (input^ in ['0'..'9']) do
```

```
      get(input);
   if eoln then
      ReadInt := false
   else
      begin
         while input^ in ['0'..'9'] do
            begin
               i := i * 10 + ord(input^) - ord('0');
               get(input)
            end;
         ReadInt := (i >= low) and (i <= high)
      end;
   readln
end; { ReadInt }
```

Tool B-6

```
{ Attempt to read a real number.  Return true and the number
   read iff successful. }
function ReadReal(var r: real): boolean;
begin
   { Note:   there is no easy way to do this in a
             portable fashion, so this implementation
             does not allow for error recovery. }
   readln(r);
   ReadReal := true
end; { ReadReal }
```

Other Osborne/McGraw-Hill Publications

An Introduction to Microcomputers: Volume 0—The Beginner's Book, 3rd Edition
An Introduction to Microcomputers: Volume 1—Basic Concepts, 2nd Edition
An Introduction to Microcomputers: Volume 3—Some Real Support Devices
Osborne 4 & 8-Bit Microprocessor Handbook
Osborne 16-Bit Microprocessor Handbook
8089 I/O Processor Handbook
CRT Controller Handbook
68000 Microprocessor Handbook
8080A/8085 Assembly Language Programming
6800 Assembly Language Programming
Z80 Assembly Language Programming
6502 Assembly Language Programming
Z8000 Assembly Language Programming
6809 Assembly Language Programming
Running Wild—The Next Industrial Revolution
The 8086 Book
PET® and the IEEE 488 Bus (GPIB), 2nd Edition
PET™/CBM™ Personal Computer Guide, 2nd Edition
CBM™ Professional Computer Guide
Business System Buyer's Guide
Osborne CP/M® User Guide
Apple II® User's Guide
Microprocessors for Measurement and Control
Some Common BASIC Programs
Some Common BASIC Programs—PET™/CBM™ Edition
Some Common BASIC Programs—Atari® Edition
Some Common BASIC Programs—TRS-80™ Level II® Edition
Some Common BASIC Programs—Apple II Edition
Practical BASIC Programs
Practical BASIC Programs—TRS-80™ Level II Edition
Practical BASIC Programs—Apple II® Edition
Practical BASIC Programs—IBM® Personal Computer Edition
Practical Pascal Programs
Payroll with Cost Accounting
Accounts Payable and Accounts Receivable
General Ledger
CBASIC™ User Guide
Science and Engineering Programs—Apple II® Edition
Interfacing to S-100/IEEE 696 Microcomputer
A User Guide to the UNIX™ System
PET™ Fun and Games
Trade Secrets: How to Protect Your Ideas and Assets
Assembly Language Programming for the Apple II®
VisiCalc®: Home and Office Companion
Discover FORTH
6502 Assembly Language Subroutines
Your ATARI® Computer
CBM™ Professional Computer Guide